Sovereign Erotics

Sovereign Erotics

A Collection of Two-Spirit Literature

Edited by

QWO-LI DRISKILL, DANIEL HEATH JUSTICE,
DEBORAH MIRANDA, AND LISA TATONETTI

The University of Arizona Press • *Tucson*

The University of Arizona Press
© 2011 The Arizona Board of Regents
All rights reserved

www.uapress.arizona.edu

Library of Congress Cataloging-in-Publication Data

Sovereign erotics : a collection of two-spirit literature / edited by Qwo-Li Driskill... [et al.].
    p.   cm.
  ISBN 978-0-8165-0242-4 (pbk.)
    1. Indian gays—Literary collections.   2. Indian lesbians—Literary collections.
3. American literature—Indian authors.   4. Gays' writings, American.   5. Indians of
North America—Sexual behavior—Literary collections.   6. American literature—
21st century.   7. Homosexuality—United States.   8. Indians of North America—
Sexual behavior.   I. Driskill, Qwo-Li.
  PS509.H57S68   2011
  810.8'0920664—dc23   2011025621

Proceeds from the purchase of this book will be donated to the Two Spirit Society of
Denver.

Manufactured in the United States of America on acid-free, archival-quality paper
containing a minimum of 30% postconsumer waste and processed chlorine free.

16   15   14   13   12   11   6   5   4   3   2   1

Contents

III: Long/Walks

IV: Wild/Flowers

Sovereign Erotics

Introduction

WRITING IN THE PRESENT

*Our hands live and work in the present, while pushing on the past. It is
impossible for us to not do both.*
    Our hands make a future.
                    —BETH BRANT, *A GATHERING OF SPIRIT*[1]

This epigraph, from Bay of Quinte Mohawk lesbian/two-spirit writer Beth
Brant's breakthrough anthology, *A Gathering of Spirit: A Collection by
North American Indian Women* (1984), characterizes the continuance
of the political and artistic labor of indigenous women in which *Sovereign Erotics: A Collection of Two-Spirit Literature* roots itself. Though too
often unacknowledged in academic circles, the creative work of Native
lesbian, bisexual, queer, and two-spirit feminists such as Brant is instrumental to Native gay, lesbian, bisexual, transgender, queer, and two-spirit
(GLBTQ2) identities and movements. This collection draws on this
model of creative resistance that elders like Brant started decades ago. We
envision this anthology as a collection of maps and stories for those who
come after and for those who may already be on their journey, but who
have journeyed without guides or fellow travelers. *Sovereign Erotics* is for
those who—like so many of us—had no role models, no one to tell us that
we were valuable human beings just as we are. This project is by and for
the People. Our hope is that this collection can push on the past while
making a contribution toward a healthier and more respectful future.

Two-spirit people—identified by many different tribally specific names
and community positions—have been living, loving, and creating art since
time immemorial. As part of this vibrant history, contemporary queer Native
literature gained public notice in the United States in the late 1970s.
In 1988, *Living the Spirit: A Gay American Indian Anthology*, the first
anthology of two-spirit literature, made a landmark debut. Though two-spirit people have continued to write, create, perform, and publish since

Living the Spirit, until now there has not been another collection published in North America that is explicitly focused on the writing and art of two-spirit people. Following the model of such important collections as *Living the Spirit,* which focused on queer Native writing, and Cherríe Moraga and Gloria Anzaldúa's *This Bridge Called My Back: Writings by Radical Women of Color* (1981), Beth Brant's *A Gathering of Spirit* (1984), Makeda Silvera's *Piece of My Heart: A Lesbian of Colour Anthology* (1991), Connie Fife's *The Colour of Resistance: A Contemporary Collection of Writing by Aboriginal Women* (1993), and Joy Harjo and Gloria Bird's *Reinventing the Enemy's Language: Contemporary Native Women's Writing of North America* (1997), which made space for two-spirit writers to be heard on their own terms, *Sovereign Erotics* will continue the work that has come before us and help clear a path for present and future generations.

Queer Native people are far from a monolithic group. We have numerous identities, artistic stances, and political agendas. We come from diverse nations, land bases, and traditions. Some of us are working to continue and/or revive understandings of gender and sexuality that are rooted in our tribal traditions. Others of us are doing work to challenge homophobia and transphobia in our communities—by "presenting ourselves" to our communities—and to challenge erasures of same-sex love and nonbinary genders within our cultural memories, regardless of the names we have (or have not) called ourselves in the past. Some of us are deeply involved with two-spirit identities, some of us are more connected to non-Native queer communities than to Native communities, and some of us see our queer identities as an irrelevant political issue within our nations. The work of artists such as Brant and the grassroots work of queer Native organizations both historically and currently have enabled us to have conversations across these differences and, we hope, imagine together a decolonized future that includes the full complexity of who we are as Native peoples.

The creative work of Native two-spirit and queer people has been central to resistance against colonial gender and sexual regimes. Organizations such as Gay American Indians (GAI) and publications by Native people such as Brant (Mohawk), Chrystos (Menominee), Janice Gould (Concow), Maurice Kenny (Mohawk), and Paula Gunn Allen (Laguna) transformed our understanding of who we are and shifted how it was possible to imagine ourselves. This collection engages these ongoing intersections and includes work by our elders—those who have cleared a path for two-spirit people to write and imagine—and work by emerging writers, whose acts of imagination have grown from seeds planted and nurtured by earlier generations of queer Native artists and activists. As a result, *Sovereign Erotics* reflects our continuance as two-spirit/queer people.

Sovereign Erotics

The notion of "sovereign erotics"—an assertion of the decolonial potential of Native two-spirit/queer people healing from heteropatriarchal gender regimes—comes from Cherokee writer Qwo-Li Driskill's 2004 essay, "Stolen from Our Bodies."[2] The theory of the erotic used here, and similarly employed in work by Chrystos, Janice Gould, Daniel Heath Justice (Cherokee Nation), Deborah Miranda (Ohlone-Costanoan Esselen Nation/Chumash), and other queer Native writers, recognizes the erotic as a "creative or generative force."[3] Justice asserts: "To ignore sex and embodied pleasure in the cause of Indigenous liberation is to ignore one of our greatest resources. It is to deny us one of our most precious gifts. Every orgasm can be an act of decolonization."[4]

The erotic, then, is not only about sexuality—though it is certainly about that—but also, as Audre Lorde has argued, about "power, used and unused, acknowledged or otherwise. The erotic is a resource within each of us that lies in a deeply female and spiritual plane. . . . In order to perpetuate itself, every oppression must corrupt or distort those various sources of power within the culture of the oppressed that can provide energy for change. For women, this has meant a suppression of the erotic as a considered source of power and information within our lives."[5] Within indigenous contexts, a return to our bodies as whole human beings can disrupt colonial gender regimes that have attempted to disavow and colonize indigenous genders and sexualities. Speaking of how the erotic visibility of Native women affects the very foundation of colonialist ideology, Miranda explains that "for Indian women to express the erotic is almost as frightening to America as if the skeletal witnesses in anthropology departments and national museums had suddenly risen from their boxes and begun to testify. The mythology of a nation built on 'discovery,' 'democracy,' and 'manifest destiny' begins to fall apart, and the old foundation, bereft of bones, cannot hold it up."[6] Driskill furthers such an idea, arguing, "I do not see the erotic as a realm of personal consequence only. Our relationships with the erotic impact our larger communities, just as our communities impact our senses of the erotic. A Sovereign Erotic relates our bodies to our nations, traditions, and histories."[7] Because the colonization of indigenous sexualities and genders is a central tactic of colonial oppression, the process of reclaiming, reinventing, and reimagining our lives as Native GLBTQ2 people is a central mode of resistance. In Miranda's words, "an indigenous erotic" is "a perpetual act of balancing—always working toward balance through one's actions, intent, and understanding of the world. But both love and the erotic are at odds with the violence and domination that structures any colonizing or patriarchal culture."[8]

Part of this resistance takes place in the act of telling our stories. This collection reflects the ways queer Native people continue to tell stories through fiction, poetry, and creative nonfiction. This work represents the diversity of writing being done by Native authors. Some of this work is both explicitly Native and two-spirit/queer, some of it focuses on Native issues without specific reference to gender or sexuality, and some of it focuses on issues of sexuality and gender and does not mark itself as "Native." Such diversity of content reflects the fact that this collection is not an ethnographic project; it is, instead, a space in which writers who identify as both "Native" and "GLBTQ2" can share their creative writing as literature, not social science.

The Question of Labels

Academia tends to be obsessed with defining terms. In ways that are not necessarily present outside of the academy, academic discourse often demands clearly defined terms in order to have a discussion. The problem, of course, is that the labels and terms communities use for themselves are often much less rigidly defined in community practice than they are within academic theory. Thus, even though the term "two-spirit" has been circulating in many Native communities for nearly two decades, we remain in a place where the term and its history need to be clearly articulated in order to have a conversation about Native GLBTQ2 identities.

In brief, "two-spirit" or "two-spirited" is an umbrella term in English that (1) refers to the gender constructions and roles that occur historically in many Native gender systems that are outside of colonial gender binaries and (2) refers to contemporary Native people who are continuing and/or reclaiming these roles within their communities. It is also often used as an umbrella term within grassroots two-spirit societies (such as the Bay Area American Indian Two-Spirits, the 2-Spirited People of the 1st Nations, the Northeast Two-Spirit Society, the Two Spirit Circle of Edmonton Society, and the Two Spirit Society of Denver) meant to be inclusive of not only those who identify as two-spirit or with tribally specific terms, but also GLBTQ Native people more broadly. As Sue-Ellen Jacobs, Wesley Thomas (Diné), and Sabine Lang point out: *"Two-spirit* (or *two-spirited*) was coined in 1990 by Native American individuals during the third Native American/First Nations gay and lesbian conference in Winnipeg. . . . with a clear intention to distance themselves from non-Native gays and lesbians" and to reject the derogatory history of the term "berdache," which "has been translated as 'kept boy' or 'male prostitute.'"[9] It is a term that comes from histories of indigenous resistance and decolonial struggles.

Not all queer Native people identify as two-spirit or see their sexualities and genders as connected to two-spirit histories in their communities, just as many people who identify as two-spirit or with tribally specific terms do not identify as gay, lesbian, bisexual, transgender, or queer. Still others identify as both GLBTQ and two-spirit but see these identities as inhabiting different social and cultural spheres, and many people shift between labels and terms depending on their contexts. Regardless of the differences that individuals may have with the term "two-spirit," it is being widely used in grassroots movements throughout the United States and Canada. Thus, the term "two-spirit" can be both an organizing tool and a particular political orientation that centralizes a decolonial agenda around issues of gender and sexuality. Within these organizations and community gatherings, people identify themselves through numerous words, including "two-spirit," "queer," "transsexual," "transgendered," "bisexual," "gay," "lesbian," "genderqueer," "intersexed," and a host of others. Though "two-spirit" originally stemmed, as Jacobs, Thomas, and Lang point out, from the desire of queer Native people to distance themselves from inaccurate terms used by anthropologists and/or from a generic GLBTQ identity that is often implicitly tied to whiteness, today "two-spirit" is not necessarily in opposition to these other identities but instead is a term meant to do distinct work and, importantly, to signify the often separate concerns of Native people. The discomfort with the term "two-spirit," for some, is in its pan-tribal and pan-historical usage. Akwesasne Mohawk poet James Thomas Stevens, for example, speaking of the term "twin-spirit," argues that the term "glosses over the many autonomous views that individual nations held concerning their queer members,"[10] while Carolyn Epple, speaking of a "Navajo framework," similarly claims that "the synthesis of nádleehí and others into a single category has often ignored variability across Native American cultures and left unexamined the relevance of gender and sexuality."[11] For other Native people, terms like "lesbian" and "queer" are seen as a part of dominant Euro-American constructions of sexuality that have little to do with more complicated gender systems in many Native traditions. In the end, what can be agreed upon is that there is no single umbrella term that can be effectively used for non-heteronormative genders and sexualities within Native communities. The terms and concepts available to us in English are all limited in their own ways. In fact, some Native people work to reject all of them, moving instead toward understanding themselves in relation to words in indigenous languages, such as "geenumu gesallagee," "mahu," "takataapui," "winkte," "hwame," "alyha," "patlatche," "nádleehí," "lhamana," "asegi," "fa'afafine," "ninauposkitzipxpe," "'aqi," and "cu'ut."

This collection reflects the complexity of identities within Native gay, lesbian, bisexual, transgender, queer, and two-spirit communities. We come from numerous histories, traditions, nations, land bases, and languages. We come from different understandings of our places in our communities, what our past has been, and what our future should be. And, as this introduction and the back-matter section "About the Contributors" recognize, we call ourselves by different names for diverse personal and/or political reasons. Perhaps what brings us together as movements and individuals, regardless of what our personal choices of identity labels may be, is a commitment to decolonial movements.

Indigenous Two-Spirit/Queer Critiques

As the publication of *Sovereign Erotics* suggests, we are in an exciting place as two-spirit people and allies. We inhabit an important moment in which the activist and artistic movements of queer Native people and the emergence of critical scholarship focused on two-spirit issues—and on critiquing colonial, heteropatriarchal gender regimes more broadly—are reaching a critical mass. Rooted in indigenous feminisms, indigenous art, the activist projects of two-spirit communities, and larger decolonial movements, activist-scholars are extending and developing what are currently being called "indigenous two-spirit/queer critiques." These critiques are ways of understanding the entwined nature of colonization and heteropatriarchy. In two-spirit/queer critiques, indigenous artists, academics, and activists, together with Native people and allies outside of the academy, imagine continued decolonial movements that center resistance to heteropatriarchy and colonial gender regimes. The recent special issue of *GLQ: A Journal of Lesbian and Gay Studies*, "Sexuality, Nationality, Indigeneity," edited by Daniel Heath Justice, Mark Rifkin, and Bethany

Schneider, as well as the collection *Queer Indigenous Studies: Critical Interventions in Theory, Politics, and Literature*, edited by Qwo-Li Driskill, Chris Finley (Confederated Tribes of the Colville Reservation), Brian Joseph Gilley (Cherokee/Chickasaw), and Scott Lauria Morgensen, reflect these indigenous two-spirit and queer critiques and function as examples of the rise in activist projects that intervene in the entwined systems of colonialism and heteropatriarchy. While the emergence of a body of critical scholarship may be recent, we want to highlight the fact that the creative work of Native GLBTQ2 people has always been unapologetically political. Work by people like Beth Brant, Chrystos, Janice Gould, and Maurice Kenny is deeply embedded within struggles for social justice. Thus, *Sovereign Erotics* is both a marker of a particular historical moment and an extension of a long history in which Native writers are also activists and scholars working to develop critical understandings and social movements.

Collaborative Process

Sovereign Erotics has more than one origin story. Qwo-Li and Daniel have known each other since their first year of undergraduate studies, while Daniel and Lisa met in November 1999 at the American Literature Association Conference on Native American Literature in Puerto Vallarta, Mexico, when they were both still in graduate school. Qwo-Li and Deborah met in the late 1990s through Native and queer literary events in the Seattle area. In 2003, Daniel, Deborah, and Lisa put together the first "Two-Spirit Studies" panel at the Native American Literature Symposium in Prior Lake, Minnesota. Out of that panel came an early bibliography of two-spirit literature and criticism that has since circulated the Web and been posted on the Association for the Study of American Indian Literatures (ASAIL) website.

At the 2005 Native American Literature Symposium in Minneapolis, Lisa and Qwo-Li talked about the fact that no collection of creative work by two-spirit people had been published since *Living the Spirit* in 1988, and they began to envision a new collection that could appear in the ambiguous future.

In 2008, Scott Lauria Morgensen approached Qwo-Li, Chris Finley, and Brian Joseph Gilley about the possibility of co-editing a scholarly collection that would include and reflect the analyses we were presenting during a panel on indigenous queer/two-spirit critiques at the Native American and Indigenous Studies Association meeting. These conversations developed into the critical collection *Queer Indigenous Studies*. In early discussions about *Queer Indigenous Studies*, Qwo-Li suggested to Scott that it would be exciting to develop two projects—one scholarly, one creative—that, together, would reflect the numerous perspectives and approaches emerging from queer Native community and scholarship. The energy from these conversations spurred Qwo-Li to invite Lisa, Daniel, and Deborah to join a second editorial collective to publish creative work by two-spirit writers, fulfilling earlier conversations between Lisa and Qwo-Li.

As these stories show, all of the editors of this collection have ongoing friendships with one another and utilize one another's creative and scholarly work. While *Queer Indigenous Studies* and *Sovereign Erotics* are separate collections, they are linked by a common origin story and inspired by emergent scholarship in indigenous queer/two-spirit critiques and the continued activist and artistic projects of two-spirit communities and individuals.

The call for *Sovereign Erotics* first circulated in summer 2008. Folks were invited to submit work in an open submission process and Qwo-Li, Daniel, Deborah, and Lisa began to spread the word to both established writers and new voices. Some established writers like Kenny and Gould committed early on; others were focused on their own new projects with no new work to spare. Sadly, some important writers, perhaps most significantly Beth Brant, could not be tracked down despite innumerable e-mail queries, snail-mail attempts to old addresses, and fruitless Web searches. Despite such disappointments, *Sovereign Erotics* developed into an incredible collection of two-spirit writing that illustrates the breadth and depth of contemporary queer Native creativity.

In acknowledgment of the diversity of authorship and content, this collection is organized into four interconnected sets of paired themes that speak to a multiplicity of experiences. As such, these structural concepts are intended as a gentle guide only.

The first, "Dreams/Ancestors," invokes the dual inspirations of the present and the past, of transformative personal vision, and of the abiding (and often hard-earned) wisdom of those who cleared the path ahead of us, sometimes in the most difficult and alienating of circumstances.

From there we move to "Love/Medicine" and the power of passion and erotic desire to tend to aching spirits and lonely hearts, to be the healing balm of a tender touch or heated embrace.

"Long/Walks" are the trails of tears, the struggles for dignity and recognition, the loneliness and alienation and shame that so many queer and two-spirited people experience when they present themselves honestly and openly to the world.

The final section, "Wild/Flowers," calls out to the wild, fierce beauty that thrives beyond the stifling confines of narrow-minded cultivation. To quote a line from Daniel's favorite Dolly Parton song, "When a flower grows wild it can always survive" ("Wildflowers," Dolly Parton, Velvet Apple Music, 1986). May this collection both honor and inspire the many loving wildflowers to bloom in full, fabulous glory, and in so doing transform this wounded world through courageous beauty.

Pushing on the Past

In the last several decades, two-spirit people have been weaving identities and communities that resist colonialism, racism, homophobia, transphobia, and sexism. This collection strives to continue the political and community-based work that anthologies such as *Living the Spirit* and *A Gathering of Spirit* began. As we have noted, there has not been another creative collection devoted to the work of Native GLBTQ2 people since *Living the Spirit* in 1988. *Sovereign Erotics* reflects major shifts, developments, and differences that have occurred since that publication.

Though any "first" is, of course, a construction that will inevitably be made obsolete as new materials come to light, at present, based on recovery work by Lisa Tatonetti, we can date contemporary writing by gay, lesbian, bisexual, transgendered/transexual, queer, and/or two-spirit Native people in North America to the mid-1970s, when Maurice Kenny published "A Night, A Bridge, A River (Beneath Brooklyn Bridge)" and "Greta Garbo" in the fall 1974 issue of *Fag Rag*, "Apache" in the June 1975 edition of the gay poetry journal *Mouth of the Dragon*, and an essay, "Tinseled Bucks: An Historical Study in Indian Homosexuality," and poem, "United," in the winter 1975/1976 issue of *Gay Sunshine: A Journal of Gay Liberation*.[12] These watershed moments stood at the rise of public awareness of both GLBTQ and American Indian activism. In 1968, the American Indian Movement (AIM) organized to fight police brutality in the streets of Minneapolis; in 1969, the Stonewall Rebellion similarly marked a stance against police harassment when New York's GLBTQ population refused to back down in the face of a police raid at the Stonewall Inn. In both cases, these landmark events made public long-standing histories of collective action and protest.

This public attention and protest marked a rise of more visible representations of activism as cries of "Gay Power" and "Red Power" became part of the civil rights landscape of the United States. While such activism represented an important challenge to dominant norms, these political movements were often marred by a lack of intersectional concerns. Thus, the gay rights movement spoke largely to the issues and interests of a white GLBTQ population, which meant that it was often characterized by both racism and sexism, while the American Indian Movement, similarly, could at times exhibit sexist, heterosexist, and homophobic tendencies. These dichotomies situated queer Native people at a crossroads in which racial, ethnic, and cultural alliances ran one way while sexuality and gender alliances ran another.

Bridging this identificational schism was one of the projects of the political organization Gay American Indians (GAI), which was founded in July 1975 by Barbara Cameron (Lakota) and Randy Burns (Paiute). In a 1976 interview with *The Advocate*, Cameron and Burns both spoke of the experiences that brought them to form GAI. Burns explained, "I was like a lot of Indian people who came to the city. During the '40s and '50s, the Bureau of Indian Affairs relocated many Indians to the cities. A lot of them were gay Indians who had 'lost' the respect of their tribes."[13]

Cameron spoke of a similar experience of alienation, saying, "My grandparents were forced to attend an eastern boarding school and had Christianity beat into them. . . . I thought, you know, that I was the only lesbian Indian in the world. Then I met my lover. I was really alienated. I felt trapped between my Indian culture and the society. That's the position of most gay Indians because it's the position of Indians as a whole. I really align myself with Indians first and gay people second."[14] The GAI was intended to alleviate such alienation. Cameron went on, "We were first and foremost a group for each other. . . . Bringing together gay Indians is our most important current task."[15]

At the same time that Cameron's and Burns's collective activism brought together America Indian people in the San Francisco community and became a beacon for the rest of the country, Kenny's landmark publications carved a place for GLBTQ2 Native people in the burgeoning literary movements of both gay and American Indian writers.

These literary movements were part of a rise of critical awareness about race, class, gender, ethnicity, and sexuality in the United States that followed on the heels of the multiple civil rights movements of the 1960s and 1970s. Cherríe Moraga and Gloria Anzaldúa's 1981 anthology, *This Bridge Called My Back: Writings by Radical Women of Color*, is widely heralded as a breakthrough text during this period. *This Bridge* is not simply a collection of the writings of women of color, even though that, too, was a rarity in the early 1980s. Instead, Moraga and Anzaldúa's collection broke ground by directly addressing the issues of racism, poverty, sexism, and homophobia. The twenty-nine contributors included a number of writers who identify either as Native — Barbara Cameron (Lakota) and Chrystos — or as Native and Latina — such as Jo Carrillo and Naomi Littlebear Morena.

As the work of writers of color radically expanded the parameters and focus of the field of "American" literature in the 1980s, so, too, did this decade herald a rise of a body of queer Native writing. Thus, many important two-spirit writers and critics published their first works during this period. In terms of her impact on the field, one of the most influential is Beth Brant. Brant's 1984 collection, *A Gathering of Spirit*, is the culmination of conversations and collaborations between women of color that were, as *This Bridge* indicates, coming into public view with the rise of 1980s multiculturalism. Brant speaks of the inception of the collection in her introduction, which is worth quoting at length:

> Jan. 3, 1982 — Montague, Massachusetts. I am visiting Michelle Cliff and Adrienne Rich, editors of *Sinister Wisdom*. We are sitting in their living room. Dinner is over. . . . We are talking about writing. About women of color writing. I ask if they had ever thought of doing an issue devoted to the writing of Indian women. They are enthusiastic, ask *me* if I would edit such a collection. There is panic in my gut. . . .
>
> As I lay in bed that night, I wrestle with this very complicated question. And I struggle with the complicated realities of my life. I am uneducated, a half-breed, a *light-skinned* half-breed, a lesbian, a feminist, an economically poor woman. Can these realities be accommodated by my sisters? By the women I expect to reach? Can I accommodate their realities? I think about responsibility, about tradition, about love. The passionate stomach-tightening kind of love I feel for my aunts, my cousins, my sister, my grandmother, my father. And so, I am told — it is time to take it on.[16]

And take it on Brant did as she gave voice through *A Gathering of Spirit* to indigenous women who were marginalized, imprisoned, straight, and queer.

Like *This Bridge*, *A Gathering of Spirit* not only included the work of indigenous women, but also explicitly addressed issues central to indigenous women's lives. Ultimately Brant's collection included among its sixty-plus contributors writing by twelve women who identified as Native lesbians: Paula Gunn Allen (Laguna), Mary Bennett (Seneca), Brant (Mohawk), Barbara Cameron (Lakota), Chrystos (Menominee), Janice Gould (Concow), Elaine Hall (Creek), Terri Meyette (Yaqui), Mary Moran (Métis), Katei Sardella (Micmac), Vickie Sears (Cherokee), and Anita Valerio (Blood/Chicana). The texts of all the writers in the anthology speak to the concerns of Native people, of Native women, examining both the joys and pain of their varied experiences. Brant explains that both she and the writers in A *Gathering of Spirit*

> want to talk about blessings, and endurance, and facing the machine. The everyday shit. The everyday joy. We make no excuses for the way we are, the way we live, the way we paint and write. We are not "stoic" and "noble," we are strong-willed and resisting.
>
> We have a spirit of rage. We are angry women. Angry at white men and their perversions. Their excessive greed and abuse of the earth, sky, and water. Their techno-christian approach to anything that lives, including our children, our people. We are angry at Indian men for their refusals of us. For their limited vision of what constitutes a strong Nation. We are angry at a so-called "woman's movement" that always seems to forget we exist. Except in romantic fantasies of earth mother, or equally romantic and dangerous fantasies about Indian-women-as-victim. Women lament our *lack* of participation in feminist events, yet we are either referred to as *et ceteras* in the naming of women of color, or simply not referred to at all. *We are not victims.* We are organizers, we are freedom fighters, we are feminists, we are healers. This is not anything new. For centuries it has been so.[17]

Brant followed her landmark anthology with her own collection of short stories, essays, and poetry, *Mohawk Trail*, in 1985. Shortly after, Chrystos published her first poetry collection, *Not Vanishing* (1988), and both Gould and Sears published their first books in 1990: Gould's poetry collection, *Beneath My Heart*, and Sears's short story collection, *Simple Songs*. In 1991, Makeda Silvera published *Piece of My Heart*. This collection was one of the first anthologies—if not the first—of creative work by lesbian, bisexual, and queer women of color living in both the United States and Canada and included writing by Susan Beaver (Mohawk, Grand River Territory), Brant, Chrystos, Connie Fife (Cree), and Victoria Lena Manyarrows (Eastern Cherokee). Fife's edited collection *The Colour of Resistance* (1993), which focuses on gender rather than sexuality, follows in Silvera's footsteps by uniting the work of straight and queer Native women on both sides of the Canadian–U.S. border and includes writing by Brant, Chrystos, Gould, and Sears among many others.

In terms of full-length fiction, Laguna author Paula Gunn Allen's 1983 *The Woman Who Owned the Shadows* was the first novel to engage a queer indigenous protagonist until Anishinaabe author Carole LaFavor's detective fiction, *Along the Journey River* (1996) and *Evil Dead Center* (1997); remarkably, a span of almost fifteen years separates these authors' works. That nearly fifteen-year span saw the slow but steady rise of two-spirit literature, as these early authors continued to publish and a new generation of writers joined their ranks.

At the same time as monographs by individual GLBTQ2 authors slowly grew in number in the 1980s, important anthologies continued to collect work by Native American writers. The earliest collections of Native literature came to print following the 1969 publication of Dakota writer Vine Deloria's *Custer Died for Your Sins: An Indian Manifesto* and Kiowa/Cherokee author N. Scott Momaday's 1969 Pulitzer Prize for his 1968 novel *House Made of Dawn*. In 1969, John R. Milton published *The American Indian Speaks*, which was a reprint of the famed 1969 *South Dakota Review* issue that focused on Native American writing. The number of small-scale press and journal compilations makes it difficult to name any single beginning, but Viking's 1974 publication of *The Man to Send Rain Clouds: Contemporary Stories by American Indians*, edited by Kenneth Rosen, is one of the earliest and best-known anthologies of Native fiction published by a mainstream press. Speaking of this period of literary production in the introduction to his own important anthology, *The Remembered Earth* (first published by Red Earth Press in 1979), Geary Hobson (Cherokee–Quapaw/Chickasaw) describes this "flurry of literary activity" as "much more than a 'boom' or a 'fad'. . . . It is a renewal, it is a continuance—and it is remembering."[18]

This focus on renewal, continuance, and memory that Hobson speaks of in *The Remembered Earth* was also clearly present in 1988 when the first and, until now, only anthology of Native literature to focus solely on two-spirit literature was published. *Living the Spirit* was compiled by the Gay American Indians (GAI), edited by white anthropologist Will Roscoe, and published by St. Martin's Press.[19] *Living the Spirit* is a remarkable anthology that arose directly out of the activism and community of GAI. The book is evidence of both the growth of GAI as an organization that, as Randy Burns, the co-founder of GAI, explained, "grew beyond our wildest dreams"[20] and the sheer depth and individuality of the talent of Native writers and artists. Following Burns's preface, the anthology is subsequently divided into three parts: (1) "Artists, Healers and Providers: The Berdache Heritage," which focuses on situating GLBTQ Native people historically; (2) "Gay American Indians Today: Living the Spirit," which includes fiction, poetry, memoir, interview, and essay; and (3) "Resources," which includes contacts for Gay American Indian organizations and HIV/AIDs services along with an extended list of "Native American Tribes with Berdache and Alternative Gender Roles." Photographs, paintings, and drawings are dispersed throughout the first two sections. The text is a powerful commentary on both the history of indigenous people who occupied diverse genders and sexualities and the voices of contemporary two-spirit people.

Living the Spirit, like the anthologies that followed it, is now a building block for future generations of writers and thinkers. Though there have been changes in terminology, the words and messages of the writers and artists in *Living the Spirit* are as relevant now as they were when they were first printed. *Sovereign Erotics* builds on this existing tradition by continuing that conversation. The threads are woven together, as the strengths of those who started it all—powerful writers like Gould and Kenny, who are in both *Living the Spirit* and *Sovereign Erotics*—blend together with the prose and poetry of a new generation of writers and activists.

Collaboratively, the pieces in *Sovereign Erotics* demonstrate not only the radical diversity between and among the voices of today's GLBTQ2 writers, but also the beauty, strength, and pride of GLBTQ2 people in the twenty-first century. This collection is certainly not a beginning, nor is it an end. It is a tool to continue imagining and building our futures together.

Notes

1. Beth Brant, *A Gathering of Spirit: A Collection by North American Indian Women* (reprint of the 1984 Sinister Wisdom Press edition, New York: Firebrand Books, 1988), 12.

2. Qwo-Li Driskill, "Stolen from Our Bodies: First Nations Two-Spirits/Queers and the Journey to a Sovereign Erotic," *SAIL: Studies in American Indian Literatures*, ser. 2.16, no. 2 (2004): 50–64.

3. Deborah Miranda, "Dildos, Hummingbirds, and Driving Her Crazy: Searching for American Indian Women's Love Poetry and Erotics," *Frontiers* 23, no. 2 (2002): 145.

4. Daniel Heath Justice, "Fear of a Changeling Moon: A Rather Queer Tale of a Cherokee Hillbilly," in *Me Sexy: An Exploration of Native Sex and Sexuality*, edited by Drew Hayden Taylor (Vancouver: Douglas & McIntyre, 2008), 106.

5. Audre Lorde, "Uses of the Erotic: The Erotic as Power," in *Sister Outsider: Essays and Speeches* (Freedom, CA: Crossing Press, 1984), 53.

6. Miranda, "Dildos, Hummingbirds, and Driving Her Crazy," 146.

7. Driskill, "Stolen from Our Bodies," 52.

8. Deborah Miranda, *The Zen of La Llorona* (Cambridge, UK: Salt Publishing, 2005), 4.

9. Sue-Ellen Jacobs, Wesley Thomas, and Sabine Lang, eds., *Two-Spirit People: Native American Gender Identity, Sexuality, and Spirituality* (Urbana: University of Illinois Press, 1997), 2–3, 4.

10. James Thomas Stevens, "Poetry and Sexuality: Running Twin Rails," *GLQ: A Journal of Lesbian and Gay Studies* 16 (2010): 184.

11. Carolyn Epple, "Coming to Terms with Navajo Nádleehí: A Critique of Berdache, 'Gay,' 'Alternate Gender,' and 'Two-Spirit,'" *American Ethnologist* 25, no. 2 (May 1998): 268.

12. There were, of course, GLBTQ2 writers who preceded Kenny, such as Cherokee playwright Lynn Riggs, as noted by Muscogee Creek/Cherokee author Craig Womack and others. What we detail here is the rise of publications by GLBTQ2 writers who openly engage GLBTQ2 themes in their work or claim a GLBTQ2 identity.

13. Quoted in Dean Gengle, "Reclaiming the Old New World: Gay Was Good with Native Americans," *The Advocate*, January 28, 1976, 40.

14. Ibid.

15. Ibid., 41.

16. Brant, *A Gathering of Spirit*, 8.

17. Ibid., 10–11.

18. Geary Hobson, "Introduction: Remembering the Earth," in *The Remembered Earth: An Anthology of Contemporary Native American Literature* (reprint of the 1979 Red Earth Press edition, Albuquerque: New Mexico Press, 1980), 1–2.

19. Contributors include Paula Gunn Allen (Laguna), Ben the Dancer (Yankton Sioux), Beth Brant (Mohawk), Chrystos (Menominee), Janice Gould (Concow), Nola M. Hadley (Métis), Maurice Kenny (Mohawk), Carole LaFavor (Ojibwa), Richard LaFortune (Yupik), Joe Lawrence Lembo (Cherokee), Daniel Little Hawk (Lakota/Southern Cheyenne/Aztec), Midnight Sun (Anishinaabe), Joe Dale Tate Nevaquaya (Comanche/Yuchi), Lawrence William O'Connor (Winnebago), Debra S. O'Gara (Tlingit), M. Owlfeather (Shoshone–Métis/Cree), Erna Pahe (Navajo), Kieran Prather (non-Indian), Will Roscoe (non-Indian), Tala Sanning (Sioux), Daniel-Harry Steward (Wintu), Mary TallMountain (Koyukon Athabascan; a straight Native ally), Hulleah Tsinhnajinnie (Navajo), and Anne Waters (Seminole/Choctaw, Chickasaw, Cherokee).

20. Randy Burns, "Preface," in *Living the Spirit: A Gay American Indian Anthology*, compiled by Gay American Indians and edited by Will Roscoe (New York: St. Martin's Press, 1988), 4.

Works Cited

Allen, Paula Gunn. *The Woman Who Owned the Shadows*. San Francisco: Aunt Lute Press, 1983.

Brant, Beth. *A Gathering of Spirit: A Collection by North American Indian Women.* Rockland, ME: Sinister Wisdom Press, 1984; reprint, New York: Firebrand Books, 1988.

———. *Mohawk Trail.* Ithaca: Firebrand Books, 1985.

Burns, Randy. "Preface." In *Living the Spirit: A Gay American Indian Anthology,* compiled by Gay American Indians and edited by Will Roscoe, 1–5. New York: St. Martin's Press, 1988.

Chrystos. *Not Vanishing.* Vancouver, BC: Press Gang Publishing, 1988.

Deloria, Vine, Jr. *Custer Died for Your Sins: An Indian Manifesto.* New York: Macmillan, 1969.

Driskill, Qwo-Li. "Stolen from Our Bodies: First Nations Two-Spirits/Queers and the Journey to a Sovereign Erotic." *SAIL: Studies in American Indian Literatures* 16, no. 2 (2004): 50–64.

Driskill, Qwo-Li, Chris Finley, Brian Joseph Gilley, and Scott Lauria Morgensen, eds. *Queer Indigenous Studies: Critical Interventions in Theory, Politics, and Literature.* Tucson: University of Arizona Press, 2011.

Epple, Carolyn. "Coming to Terms with Navajo Nádleehí: A Critique of Berdache, 'Gay,' 'Alternate Gender,' and 'Two-Spirit.'" *American Ethnologist* 25, no. 2 (May 1998): 267–290.

Fife, Connie, ed. *The Colour of Resistance: A Contemporary Collection of Writing by Aboriginal Women.* Toronto: Sister Vision Press, 1993.

Gay American Indians, comp., and Will Roscoe, ed. *Living the Spirit: A Gay American Indian Anthology.* New York: St. Martin's Press, 1988.

Gengle, Dean. "Reclaiming the Old New World. Gay Was Good with Native Americans." *The Advocate,* January 28, 1976, 40–41.

Gould, Janice. *Beneath My Heart: Poetry.* Ithaca: Firebrand Books, 1990.

Green, Rayna. *That's What She Said: Contemporary Poetry and Fiction by Native American Women.* Bloomington: Indiana University Press, 1984.

Harjo, Joy, and Gloria Bird, eds. *Reinventing the Enemy's Language: Contemporary Native Women's Writing of North America.* New York: Norton, 1997.

Hobson, Geary, ed. *The Remembered Earth: An Anthology of Contemporary Native American Literature.* Albuquerque: Red Earth Press, 1979; reprint, Albuquerque: New Mexico Press, 1980.

Jacobs, Sue-Ellen, Wesley Thomas, and Sabine Lang, eds. *Two-Spirit People: Native American Gender Identity, Sexuality, and Spirituality.* Urbana: University of Illinois Press, 1997.

Justice, Daniel Heath. "Fear of a Changeling Moon: A Rather Queer Tale of a Cherokee Hillbilly." In *Me Sexy: An Exploration of Native Sex and Sexuality,* edited by Drew Hayden Taylor, 87–108. Vancouver: Douglas & McIntyre, 2008.

Justice, Daniel Heath, Mark Rifkin, and Bethany Schneider, eds. *GLQ: A Journal of Lesbian and Gay Studies,* "Sexuality, Nationality, Indigeneity" 16.1–2 (2010).

Kenny, Maurice. "Apache." *Mouth of the Dragon* 5 (June 1975): n.p.

———. "Greta Garbo." *Fag Rag* 10 (fall 1974): 27.

———. "A Night, A Bridge, A River (Beneath Brooklyn Bridge)." *Fag Rag* 10 (fall 1974): 8.

———. "Tinseled Bucks: An Historical Study in Indian Homosexuality." *Gay Sunshine: A Journal of Gay Liberation* 26–27 (winter 1975/1976): 15–17.

——. "United." *Gay Sunshine: A Journal of Gay Liberation* 26–27 (winter 1975/1976): 17.

LaFavor, Carole. *Along the Journey River: A Mystery.* Ithaca: Firebrand Books, 1996.

——. *Evil Dead Center: A Mystery.* Ithaca: Firebrand Books, 1997.

Lorde, Audre. "Uses of the Erotic: The Erotic as Power." In *Sister Outsider: Essays and Speeches,* 53–59. Freedom, CA: Crossing Press, 1984.

Milton, John R., ed. *The American Indian Speaks.* Vermillion: Dakota Press, University of South Dakota, 1969.

Miranda, Deborah A. "Dildos, Hummingbirds, and Driving Her Crazy: Searching for American Indian Women's Love Poetry and Erotics." *Frontiers* 23, no. 2 (2002): 135-149.

——. *The Zen of La Llorona.* Cambridge, UK: Salt Publishing, 2005.

Momaday, N. Scott. *House Made of Dawn.* New York: Harper & Row, 1968.

Moraga, Cherríe, and Gloria Anzaldúa. *This Bridge Called My Back: Writings by Radical Women of Color.* New York: Kitchen Table Press, 1981.

Rosen, Kenneth, ed. *The Man to Send Rain Clouds: Contemporary Stories by American Indians.* New York: Viking Press, 1974.

Sears, Vickie. *Simple Songs: Stories.* Ithaca: Firebrand Books, 1990.

Silvera, Makeda. *Piece of My Heart: A Lesbian of Colour Anthology.* Toronto: Sister Vision, 1991.

Stevens, James Thomas. "Poetry and Sexuality: Running Twin Rails." *GLQ: A Journal of Lesbian and Gay Studies* 16 (2010): 183–189.

PART ONE

Dreams/Ancestors

Paula Gunn Allen

Some Like Indians Endure

i have it in my mind that
dykes are indians

they're a lot like indians
they used to live as tribes
they owned tribal land
it was called the earth

they were massacred
lots of times
they always came back
like the grass
like the clouds
they got massacred again

they thought caringsharing
about the earth and each other
was a good thing
they rode horses
and sang to the moon

but i don't know
about what was so longago
and it's now that dykes
make me think i'm with indians
when i'm with dykes

because they bear
witness bitterly
because they reach
and hold
because they live every day
with despair laughin
in cities and country places
because earth hides them
because they know
the moon

because they gather together
enclosing
and spit in the eye of death

indian is an idea
some people have
of themselves
dyke is an idea some women
have of themselves
the place where we live now
is idea
because whiteman took
all the rest
because daddy
took all the rest
but the idea which
once you have it
you can't be taken
for somebody else
and have nowhere to go
like indians you can be
stubborn

the idea might move you on,
ponydrag behind
taking all your loves and
children maybe downstream
maybe beyond the cliffs
but it hangs in there
an idea

like indians
endures

it might even take your
whole village with it
stone by stone
or leave the stones
and find more
to build another village
someplace else

like indians
dykes have fewer and fewer
someplace elses to go
so it gets important to know
about ideas and
to remember or uncover
the past
and how the people
traveled
all the while remembering
the idea they had
about who they were
indians, like dykes
do it all the time

dykes know all about dying
and that everything belongs
to the wind
like indians
they do terrible things
to each other
out of sheer cussedness
out of forgetting
out of despair

so dykes
are like indians
because everybody is related
to everybody
in pain
in terror

in guilt
in blood
in shame
in disappearance
that never quite manages
to be disappeared
we never go away
even if we're always
leaving

because the only home
is each other
they've occupied all
the rest
colonized it: an
idea about ourselves is all
we own

and dykes remind me of indians
like indians dykes
are supposed to die out
or forget
or drink all the time
or shatter
go away
to nowhere
to remember what will happen
if they don't

they don't anyway—even
though the worst happens
they remember and they
stay
because the moon remembers
because so does the sun
because the stars
remember
and the persistent stubborn grass
of the earth

Los Angeles, 1981

Kim Shuck

Warrior

for Carol Lee, and the rest of us

There are bullets hiding in the trees near the creek.
They could be from any one of three wars,
Various skirmishes
Or the one massacre.
The residue of a failure to communicate
Lies invisible in the landscape.
The trees grow roots in patterns
That spell stories of lead and hiding lead.
We don't get to tell the trees how they feel about war,
And a massacre with hydroxyls and carbon chains
Helped by
Twisted metal or
An iced road.
Even the water is in on it.
It's more than mourning
You are the smoke of a fire
Lit from my burning hair
Soldiers might bless their weapons in that smoke.
I might have been a soldier myself
And you
A news photo
Symbol
Or smoke.
War trophy

Prisoner of war
Justification.
We might organize
Send jackets
Canned food
Powdered milk.
We might publish our objection
Burn our own offerings
Learn to carry a gun.
We might throw rocks
Light candles
Sing songs,
Enact other forms of cosmetic surgery.
How about this:
Help me pull the bullets from the trees.
Learn my language
I'll learn your history.

Indira Allegra

Vessel

Girl child use a bowl to play divination
a calabash yawns tobacco colors

Mama pours soup into the bowl
steam, then the letters appear
          *
Grandma had wanted to be cremated
with her ashes scattered on the ocean
"It the quickest way back
to where we come from" she had said
a stern cigar burning down
in the corner of her mouth
that was two weeks ago
          *
Girl child holds her breath
squeezes her eyes shut
black braids sway soft
dips the spoon in murmuring
child songs and looks at letters
she speaks and Mama pales
"Mama, what this mean?
I   H   E   R   E."

Joel Waters

Kid Icarus

Every Indian has a silver lining
I thought to myself
As I saw a young skin
Trying to fly
Near downtown Pine Ridge
Amidst all the dirt clouds
He had speckles of silver paint
Around his mouth
And zeppelins
That were his fingertips
Making zigzags
Across the air
But he was going nowhere
I'd thought had the spray paint
Been gold
He'd be Icarus
Befittingly burnt by the sun

What mangy wings we have
Unable to get off the ground
Without a wicked substance
We are the meek
But we will not inherit a thing
Even if we could rise

With our degenerated bones
Most of us around here know
It's a no-fly zone
How amazing
Those golden gates must be
But I cannot imagine standing
On a white cloud
Tracking mud into heaven
I would never be let in
Perhaps I should've run to
That Gabriel-like Indian
Blowing into his plastic
Bag trumpet
Perhaps I should've kissed him
It'd be the closest I'd ever get
To taste the sweet vapors
Of a Heaven

Craig Womack

The King of the Tie-snakes

Josh Henneha, Eufaula, Oklahoma, 1972
from Drowning in Fire *(2001)*

I spent my days that Oklahoma summer fishing with my grandfather or traipsing after my cousin and his friends through hills covered with black-jacks and post oaks, cicadas humming in my ears, chiggers at my ankles, following as they scouted dark places to smoke their cigarettes and gather their secrets. My cousin, Lenny Henneha, barely tolerated me, the ties of blood hardly enough to admit a sissy into his circle. This resentful inclusion was a step up, actually, from school, where I spent my days on the edge of the playground, watching the scrabbling bodies weave in and out, frenetic blurs of girls jumping rope, clumps of boys playing soccer, bobbing up and down over a lake of asphalt. As for me, I waited for the misery to end when the bell would proclaim relief, when the teacher would call roll, singing out "Josh," and I would at least have the comfort of hiding behind a book back in class, its hard cover held before me like a Jesuit missionary's crucifix. But that was another world, and I had two more months left of sweating and barely being able to breathe the dripping Oklahoma air before returning to school in the fall.

"I can't swim out that far," Josh said, shaking while beads of water ran off his chin and dripped onto his chest. He had started out toward the raft and turned back, the other boys urging him on, already halfway out in the lake. He stood ankle deep in a mossy bed of lake weeds under a bright blue sky, his shoulders sunburned and peeling. He turned, climbed out of the weeds, and headed up the embankment in the direction of the dam.

"You fuckin' pussy," Sammy Barnhill hollered from the lake at Josh's retreating form as he made the blacktop road at the top of the hill.

"Come on, Josh," Lenny yelled in exasperation. "We ain't taking you anywhere else with us."

Josh shrugged and kept walking.

It was Jimmy Alexander's turn. "It ain't that far. Look, you can swim out on that intertube." Jimmy pointed at the boat dock where the black tube was swollen on the top of the hot concrete steps. Josh paused and considered Jimmy's advice. Before long he had the tube untied, dipped on both sides in the water to cool it off, and he was kicking his way toward the others, the willow trees leaning over the lakeshore becoming farther away each time he cast a backward glance, the dam road at the top of the hill a distant blur, the Texaco station in front of the dirt access road that led down to the lake now invisible as he kicked through the water, the sun burning overhead.

He and the boys swam out toward the old raft anchored off the shore of Lake Eufaula, racing to see who could get there first. Sammy pulled himself over the moss-covered sides, and, one by one, as the boys tried to grab onto the ladder and climb aboard, he kicked them back into the water. He announced, "Let's play king of the raft." As Sammy defended the ladder, Jimmy swam to the other side and hopped aboard. Josh, floating on his inner tube on the opposite side, watched Jimmy coming up out of the water. As Jimmy pulled himself aboard he seemed to rise out of the lake in an unending succession; his wiry arms and upper body kept coming and coming, followed by his swimming trunks and long legs, like a snake uncoiling. He was taller than the rest of them. Jimmy's eyes met Josh's just before Jimmy stood fully erect on the slippery wooden planks. Jimmy quickly turned away and snuck over to where Sammy stood, occupied with kicking Lenny back into the water, and Jimmy shoved Sammy into the lake. "New king," he said to Sammy, who came up spitting water and calling Jimmy a motherfucker.

Jimmy grew tired of using his superior size to keep Sammy off the raft, and he pretended not to notice Sammy mouthing off. Jimmy was shaking water out of his ears when Sammy climbed back up. The raft pitched a little, and Jimmy lost his balance, falling to his knees.

"Dumb nigger," Sammy taunted. Jimmy grabbed Sammy's ankles and sent him sprawling on his ass. He landed with a loud *thunk*. Jimmy stood above Sammy. Jimmy's short-cropped hair glistened in the sun, and he seemed to Josh bathed in light after emerging from the murky lake. Jimmy was more mature than the rest of the boys, the athlete of the bunch, a basketball player obsessed with the Lakers and his hero, Kareem Abdul-Jabbar. Jimmy, like many Creeks, had black blood and features, a fact the other boys held against him and used to discredit him since he could beat them at sports. Josh pretended to watch a ski boat passing by, back and forth, but he was using each opportunity to check out Jimmy, who was now lying back, hands folded behind his head, taking in the sun. The water was drying on Jimmy's chest in mottled streaks that ran down his belly to his swimming trunks, an old pair that was missing a button, pinned at the top instead.

Josh had secret words with special powers. Each time he followed the ski boat's pass between the raft and the shore, and his eyes swept over Jimmy, Josh sent out another message. The way it worked was that only the right person would know he was receiving the thoughts that Josh had stored up inside his head. Not very many people would know what the words meant. In the wrong hands the message could be deadly, or the recipient might turn on him. Josh watched Jimmy for a sign that the signals had registered, but nothing seemed to be happening.

Josh carefully unknotted a plastic bag, which contained inside it another knotted plastic bag, which he also undid, retrieving its contents.

"You brought a book with you?" Sammy said scornfully.

"Give him a break, man," Jimmy said. "What you reading, anyway?" Josh held up the cover. Jimmy squinted, reading the title, *The Happy Hollisters*, then laughed. "What do you get out of a story like that?" he asked. Josh couldn't explain that the Happy Hollisters were so far away, and he took comfort in that. Jimmy let it drop when Lenny interrupted by pointing out a school of crappie darting up to the raft's ladder.

Josh knew the sting of being last at everything. During school recess, Miss Manier, whom the boys all called Miss Manure, would have the kids line up to choose teams for kickball. Each day she would send one of the girls over to fetch Josh from his lone perch near the tetherball poles. Miss Manier began by saying, "Okay, children. Which one of you boys wants to volunteer for team captain?" One of the more athletic guys, usually Jimmy, would speak up first and stand there with his hand up in the air. But Miss Manier always picked a white boy to lead the teams. And next time Jimmy would volunteer again. Josh wondered why Jimmy didn't give up after a while. Didn't he get it? Alone, Josh dreamed of advising Jimmy about the ways of Miss Manier, inviting Jimmy over to his house where Josh would take him up to his room. Jimmy would sit on Josh's bed, and Josh would sit at his desk and say, "Jimmy, what you wanna do is watch close while captains are being picked. You might notice that Raymond gets picked every time, and he hates being team captain. Wait until we get out on the field, and offer to be last up if Raymond will let you lead the team because Raymond lives to bat." Jimmy would clap Josh on the shoulder and say, "Thanks, buddy, I never thought of that." Maybe afterward they would lie on Josh's bed, and Josh would casually pull out a *Sports Illustrated* with Kareem on the cover, and Jimmy would pick it up and explain to Josh all the mysteries of basketball.

Or Jimmy would toss Josh a ball lying in the corner of the room. "Hold it like this," he'd say, walking over and standing behind Josh. "Here, put your middle finger over the air valve," he'd add while helping Josh position his hands, and they would both slowly raise the ball together, time and time again, until Josh had it down perfect.

Out on the playground, Josh wondered why Miss Manier didn't just have them number off and separate into teams, sparing them all the daily humiliation. What was her game? But she was a white lady, so who knows? Not only did Josh never get picked for team captain, since he was Indian, but he got chosen just after the last boy was picked and before the first girl, because he was the least athletic of the schoolboys. Miss Manier never did anything to stop the girls from being picked last, either. She pretended not to notice any of this. Or maybe she really didn't see it. Hard to say. She looked busy pushing her glasses farther up on her nose when she wanted not to hear or see things.

The boys called him faggot. All the time. Every day. It might be summer vacation, but there was no vacation from that, and it had become like a second name; "Josh faggot" was as familiar to him as "Josh Henneha." He couldn't understand their world, either, whether they hated him because he read books or because he "walked like a girl," which they chanted to him in singsong voices on the bus rides home. Would it be any better in seventh grade? On the playground, Josh liked playing the girls' games because he didn't have to endure the burning shame of choosing teams. The girls simply took turns playing hopscotch or tetherball, and he felt more comfortable apart from the boys' cutthroat competition. During recess, when the kids could play with whomever they wanted, he knew that none of them would choose him for their team anyway. So he either joined the girls or stood alone at the edge of the blacktop watching the others.

Jimmy took a lot of shit for sometimes putting up with Josh. When Sammy would see Jimmy talking to Josh, he would say, "Jimmy, now we know. You're one of them, too. We see you got a new little girlfriend." Occasionally, Jimmy would convince the boys to let Josh throw in with them, although they complained about having him in their presence. Josh would join them only after relentless teasing. "You pussy. Playing with the girls again? Want to borrow my sister's panties?"

Today, though, Josh had figured out a way of making himself useful to Jimmy. From the bread bag, Josh pulled out Jimmy's pack of cigarettes, which he'd tied inside with his book before they swam out. Josh handed the pack to Jimmy. Jimmy passed each member of the gang one of them, and he demonstrated his awe-inspiring ability to light up even on the windiest days by holding the match with his thumb and forefinger and cupping his hand around the burning flame. Smokes were important, and Josh had managed to get them out to the middle of Lake Eufaula, an accomplishment that no one on the raft could deny. He'd used his head, he thought, even if none of them would admit it.

Lenny spoke up. "Let's have a diving contest." The first one to bring up a rock from the bottom of the lake would win, he explained.

The boys argued about who would go first. Josh sat alone on the edge of the raft staring wistfully, trancelike, over the side, his feet dangling in the water. They chose the diving order. Sammy would take the first turn, of course, then Jimmy and Lenny. They all agreed that Josh would go last, since, as Sammy said all the time, "He ain't no count nohow." Josh said, "You go ahead. I don't feel like diving just now." They met his statement with the usual jeers describing Josh's mother, words about unmentionable acts performed on close kin and the family dog, comments about his female relatives' sexual activities with ancient white men in overalls who sat on the town bench in Eufaula by the old Palmers Grocery and spat long streams of tobacco juice, and concluded with the final touch, without which any string of insults lacked finality: "I bet you're chicken, faggot."

Josh had an idea. He thought, "I'll see if Jimmy can receive my messages from beneath the water. I'll count to three after he dives and begin transmitting. I'll call to him from on top of the raft; Jimmy will answer back from below the waves. Maybe if I can't send my thoughts when we're sitting so close together, what about when I'm above the surface, and he's below?" It could be that brain waves can only be sent from opposite worlds, and only received if Jimmy is underwater, cut off from air and sunlight, blindly making his way deeper and deeper toward the sunken realms where big cats and largemouth bass lay hidden in sinkholes under fallen submerged tree trunks. When Jimmy returned and opened his hand, the rock would be a sign.

Sammy began the ritual by giving a sermon on deep-diving techniques. "You have to blow all your air out," he said, "and make your ears pop."

Then, plugging his nose like a sailor jumping from the heights of a sinking battleship, he leaped, penetrating the surface and sending out waves that lightly rocked the raft. Feet first, the wrong way, Josh thought, if you wanna reach bottom. But he didn't say anything. The boys peered down into the light reflecting off the surface of the lake and tensed as they waited for Sammy to come back up. Finally, a hand shot from beneath the water, and Sammy's clenched fist broke through the glassy film, projecting toward the blue sky.

Sammy, pale and shaking from barely having enough air to make it back up, climbed onto the raft and didn't say a word in spite of the others' questions. "Did you reach bottom?" they asked. After he caught his breath, Sammy slowly opened his fist and proclaimed that he had dropped the rock shortly before reaching the surface. This explanation burned in Josh's ears.

"I'm going next," Josh said suddenly. He looked like he had just awakened from a long sleep. The boys looked quizzically at one another, wondering why Josh, who usually responded only at the last minute to their dares, took it upon himself to be one of the first divers. But Josh just had to go now. When Jimmy entered the lake waters, Josh wanted to have his dive over with so he could devote all his concentration to transmitting his message to Jimmy rather than having to worry about whether or not he would be the one to emerge with the rock.

Josh had listened attentively to Sammy's sermon on diving, but he jumped headfirst into the lake, unlike Sammy, then he blew the air from his lungs and pushed as hard as he could with his legs, grabbing desperately at the water, pulling himself down farther. He would finally show them. Maybe he couldn't kick a ball over second base, but he would come back out of the water with that rock, and he pictured shooting above the surface with it in his hand as the boys stared in amazement. He would climb the ladder one-handed, all the while holding the prize above his head like he had just won a new world title. He wouldn't say anything, just set the rock in the center of the raft and step back and smirk like he thought nothing of retrieving rocks from twenty feet below. Leading the contest would allow him to insist that Jimmy go right after him, bringing them even closer to each other's secrets, ready for Josh's messages. Maybe he and Jimmy would be the only ones to make it from the lake's depths with something to show for themselves, and they'd be united as winners. His lungs burned for air as he pushed deeper and deeper through the murky water, but he kept the image of claiming his victory before his eyes, urging himself on because it was a test, and his messages to Jimmy depended on it.

His hand struck soft mud. He couldn't believe he'd actually made it when even Sammy hadn't been able to reach bottom. He felt around until he clutched a slimy, moss-covered rock. He held it to his chest with one hand, embracing it like a mother holding her child, and he began grabbing at the water with his free hand and kicking his feet.

He broke the surface and gasped, but his hand had struck something solid just above his head, and he heard the thump resound like the inside of a kettle drum. He pulled in mouthfuls of air, but they smelled of dank mold. When he opened his eyes, he saw darkness, and he felt confusion, like having awakened in the middle of the night not knowing where he was. He wanted to call out, but he knew that would make him look chicken and spoil the effect of having retrieved the stone. He began to hyperventilate and panic, and the thought of winning the contest left him, replaced with the fear of surfacing in this unexpected world, breathing in darkness. He heard the voices of the boys above, and, finally, it dawned on him. He had come up under the raft. The others were sitting one foot above him and didn't even know it. They must have been busy chattering and not heard his hand strike the raft's bottom. He felt his way to the edge, ready to duck under and surface on the other side to show the boys his rock and claim his rights as winner.

Then he stopped. A single thought flashed through his mind and seemed to come from somewhere outside himself. "What if I just stay here? For like five minutes? Then when I come up, with the rock in my hand, I'll have proven I can stay underwater longer than anyone, beyond anything Sammy can explain. I won't tell them how I did it. And when I send Jimmy under, he'll be ready to believe my powers."

During those fishing trips with my grandfather at Lake Eufaula, I learned to row our old aluminum boat a little ways offshore and drop the cement coffee-can anchor while he got the poles ready. He was rigging up a pole he'd given my father for his birthday, but my father wasn't much to fish. "Don't tell Dad I never use this," my father had cautioned me when I left the house with the pole to go over to Grandpa's that morning. Grandpa would set things up in the boat before we got started. This arrangement seemed to work best since he easily became grouchy when he had to tell me which lures to try, how to work them in the water, and what to put on my line when I wasn't having any luck. The third time out he had snapped at me, "How many times I gotta tell you don't tie on a leader to that plastic worm." He spoke a kind of broken English I'd heard many of the old people use around there, especially on the days he complied with my grandma's prodding to go to the Indian Baptist church. At Grandma's church the deacon seated you in some kind of hierarchy I didn't quite understand, but it had to do with length of membership since the oldest people were in the front. The deacon would point his cane to the proper pew, directing men to one side, women to the other. The sermon was in Creek, little of which I understood, and afterward, when Grandma's friends came up to visit, they would speak English since I was from the younger generation. But I took it that Grandpa cared a good deal more for fishing than churchgoing.

After we got settled on the plank benches on our respective sides of the boat, he handed me my pole rigged with a bobber and minnow. He had given up teaching me how to jig the bass lure through the water and had given me over as a useless case, destined to use live bait forever. Which is the way most Indian guys fished anyway, my grandpa always complained, one hand on the pole, the other on the Budweiser. My grandpa, for some reason, had mastered all the nuances of bass fishing rather than just slinging a bobber with stink bait underneath it out into the lake. So I sat, elbow on knee, chin in hand, watching the red-and-white sphere appear and reappear in the waves of shimmering water, imagining it as a boat approaching a distant shore and I had stood years on the beach awaiting the return of someone on board. One day I had brought a book to read while I waited for a fish to strike, but Grandpa had glared at me with such disdain that I had timidly put it back in my lunch sack. I didn't say anything, but I pouted all morning. I was rereading all of C. S. Lewis's *Narnia* books and was completely taken with the notion of a wardrobe that was a closet on one side and a world of talking animals on the other, and the boy who could go get his brothers and sisters and bring them back with him, if only they'd believe.

Grandpa could cast his lure, send it singing in an arcing loop out across the lake, land it with a soft *ker-plop* over by a stump where he said the bass were, and reel it in, working it at the same speed with a gentle tugging motion that made it snake through the water. But what was really beyond belief was his ability to talk during these adroit maneuvers. When he spoke, all his words led up to a story; all conversation was a prelude. So I wasn't surprised when he said to me, "Hey, how 'bout it, this lake pretty big mess of water, ain't it?"

It was huge; even had we owned a motorboat, it would have taken hours, I imagined, or days, to boat all the way around it. "I used to farm right over yonder," he said, nodding toward the middle of the lake. "Before the dam went in. Built it in '63, I think it was. Started gathering water in '64.

Now, water's all over. Little cotton, little corn, I growed some of every-thing, few hogs, too. Yep, had a house, right over thataway. Your daddy was borned there. Now you can't get nowhere around here on the same roads you used to. All covered up."

I was fascinated by the thought of underwater farms, barns, houses, pas-tures, and I could see kitchens with families of bass and crappie darting in and out the windows and under the legs of dining room tables.

"There is something white man has never saw or caught," he went on, "something in the water. Their head is shape like a deer. If you are by water it has a power and will pull you in. It don't pull just anyone in water, just certain people. If you ever see a whirling water in the river you better get out of there. It makes a sound like a big snake then rises up on a sheet of water. If you ever see the strange monster, someone dies. White man never did catch this tie-snake. They have horns like a deer and all kinds of color, kinda greenish and red. Long time ago, the old Indian medicine doctor use to make them things come out and catch them. When they catch them, they use to cut the ends off their horns and hunt with them. They would throw something doctored with Indian medicine, throw it in four times in the whirling water, and make tie-snake come out. One time my daddy said he went fishing and he kinda got a funny feeling by the river, like scared, and pretty soon he heard a growling sound in water and after a while it started bubbling so he got out of there fast. I heard he told about it. It was near Gaines Creek south of here."

Grandpa reeled his line in and tied on a new spinner. I had been dan-gling my arm over the side of the boat. I pulled it back in. Grandpa started back up. "One man name Curtis Goolman, kin of yours, he told me one time. . . ."

"I bet he's got the rock in his hand right now," laughed Jimmy. Sammy threw in, "Naw, he's probably got something else in his hand." All the boys laughed. Thirty more seconds passed, and a smothering silence fell over them. The boys began to take deep drags on their cigarettes and looked down at their bare toes. They coughed nervously and listened to the water slapping the sides of the raft. Sammy tried to kill time by blowing smoke rings, but the wind swept them out over the water.

Finally, Lenny spoke. "What do y'all s'pose happened to him?"

"I think we ought to swim to shore," Sammy said coolly.

"We don't know for sure if he drowned. We can't just leave him here," said Jimmy. "We gotta at least stay until we know what happened."

"What are we gonna tell everybody when we get home?" said Sammy. "We better get our stories straight or his folks are liable to blame us. It ain't our fault the dickhead can't swim." The other boys looked over at Sammy and saw that they were supposed to laugh again.

Jimmy said, "I'm staying here for a spell. Not that I'm afraid of getting in trouble or anything. I just wanna see if maybe he comes back up." Lenny sided with Jimmy and decided to stay on the raft. Sammy said, "Well, while y'all are sitting here getting cold in the wind, I'll be stretched out in the sun on the bank." Sammy slid into the water, and swam for shore.

Baa-rump. Baa-rump. Baa-rump. Under the raft, Josh heard the buoy bumping against it up above, steady as a heartbeat, and thought that he had better come back up before he stretched his miraculous powers too thin and the boys went home, leaving him for drowned. Then he wouldn't get to test his secret messages to Jimmy.

Josh dived and ducked under the raft. Just before he broke the surface, he felt a sudden tug on his leg. A clump of fishing line had wrapped around his ankle, and when he swam up he had pulled all the slack out, binding the entangled mesh tightly. He felt with his hands, unable to see in the murky water. The other end of the line was twisted around the cable that anchored the raft to the bottom. He dropped the rock. Had it been a single strand of line, he could have broken it easily since fishermen used light test weights for the bass and crappie in the lake. But with the whole clump wound around itself, the strength of the line was greatly magnified. Each tug dug into the flesh of his ankle with a sharp little searing that he couldn't exactly call pain. He almost wanted to laugh, then, panic-stricken, he placed both feet against the cable and pulled with his hands.

Josh strained and jerked. "Oh God! No. Please. Let me get loose. I won't try another trick like this," he thought, as he pulled at the line. He started to cry out in terror and swallowed some water. He began to choke and cough, fighting to keep holding his breath. He cut his palms on the thin strands, and, in desperation, he felt around, sightless in the murky water, to locate the individual strands. He began breaking them one by one. He had torn apart five or six of them when something brushed past his chest. Josh felt his arms flailing in the water around him. He opened his eyes and saw the underwater city where he was tethered to the spokes of somebody's wagon wheel parked on the street in front of a building. A large channel catfish with a Fu Manchu mustache was swimming in place just between the top porch rail and the roof of the building, making underwater

burbling noises that sounded like garbled words. The fish darted inside
the front window, and Josh watched him enter. A painted sign above the
door stoop read:

GRAYSON BROS
DEALERS
IN
GENERAL MERCHANDISE

Josh could hear the catfish inside the store singing a jingle about seed, har-
nesses, farm machinery, groceries, "not to mention," he sang, "traveler's
supplies, prints, hosiery, boots, shoes, hats, caps, and all the etceteras req-
uisite to a first-class Western business house."

Josh looked down at his leg. A balled-up coil of snakes had wrapped
themselves around him, from ankle to knee, and they moved in and out of
each other, swaying in the lake bottom current and weaving between the
wagon spokes. Just when they felt like they had loosened their grip on him,
he'd pull and they'd tighten back up. He had gone off to the underwater
world, but he couldn't get back to his . . . *the bathtub water drains slowly
down and I feel my body grow heavier Lucy scrubs my back the warm water
goes galump galump galump down the drain as she blows the smoke in my
ear in the beginning we were covered we were covered we were covered don't
go near swirling water they got horns that make powerful medicine the bub-
bles this is a trade I'm trading my air for water air for water water for air it's
not fair that rhymes water is heavier than air but they are both free we were
covered by a mighty fog in her lap kicking that ball clean over third base out
over the chain-link fence off over the housetops and Jimmy cheering while
I run those bases at a slow dogtrot and he makes hook shots from center court
those slimy bastards will wish they would have picked me first look at the
bubbles it's not a fair trade air for water breathing smoke into me covered
by a mighty fog and hold on to each other so they don't get lost I'll hold on
to Jimmy and maybe he'll wanna hold on to me too if he gets my message.*

On top of the raft, Jimmy shouted, "Oh my God. Look at all the bub-
bles coming up!" He jumped to his feet and pointed toward the water. He
leaned over the raft and noticed the tugging was coming from beneath,
not from the waves. "It looks like he's just below the surface." Jimmy dove
headfirst toward the troubled water. Josh saw a snake, with horns, swim-
ming toward him. Jimmy bumped into Josh after having just barely bro-
ken water. The giant snake was trying to wrap itself around Josh, and he
was too weak to stop it. Jimmy placed both arms around Josh's chest and

tried to swim back up, but he couldn't budge him. He followed the length of Josh's body with his hands, feeling everywhere until finally reaching the entangled mesh of line around Josh's ankle. Jimmy popped above the waves and pulled himself back on the raft, shakily grabbing a pocketknife they kept stuck in the wood planks for fishing. Jimmy dove back below, grabbing handfuls of knotted line, and he kept sawing through whole bunches of the mesh. Finally he felt Josh drifting away as he sawed through the last of it. He grabbed him again below the arms and swam toward the raft.

Josh was awkward and heavy, and his legs and arms flopped limply while Jimmy pushed him against the ladder, keeping him in place by standing on the bottom rung and holding him with one arm and pressing against him with his body. Lenny grabbed Josh's arms while Jimmy shoved from behind. They pulled him onto the middle of the raft, where Josh lay pale and motionless. Jimmy kneeled over him. He hoped Lenny wouldn't notice his hands shaking. He tried to control his voice, but he got dizzy and thought for a moment he might pass out. "You know how to do that mouth-to-mouth thing they taught us at school?"

"I ain't kissing no guy," Lenny said. "Let's just swim back and get help."

"He'll die, you fucking idiot," Jimmy said. "You're going to help me right now!" He grabbed Lenny by the shoulders and slammed him down by Josh's side. "Just help me keep his head tilted back," he said. Jimmy leaned over Josh, plugged his nose, and boosted his head up, then began breathing into him. Lenny stared in horror at Josh's strange, pallid hue. "What are we gonna do?" he whimpered. "I wish we had never swam out here. Oh, God, I hope this works."

Josh coughed, and his body began to twitch. He threw up all over himself, and he rolled over on his side and started spitting out mouthfuls of water. Jimmy and Lenny threw lake water on him to rinse him off. Josh just lay there and sucked in big gulps of air. The two boys stared down at him. The color started to come back to his flesh, his skin returning to brown. "Do you reckon he can talk? I never seen anyone drown before," Lenny said.

"I don't know," Jimmy said. "Josh. Say something."

"I had it. Dropped it. Really, I had it in my hand," he sputtered.

"Sure you did, buddy. You almost drowned. We thought you were a goner. Josh, can you swim back? Um, I mean me and Lenny could help you if you need us to," Jimmy said. Josh tried to stand, but his legs crumpled underneath him, and he sagged back down to the floor of the raft.

Lenny helped Josh stand up. He placed one arm around his side and slowly pulled him to his feet. Lenny draped Josh's arm over his shoulder and helped him stand while Jimmy climbed down the ladder and stood on the bottom rung in the water. They helped Josh over the side. Jimmy wrapped his arm around Josh and said, "We'll take turns swimming him to shore." Jimmy started out, holding Josh with one arm while swimming on his side. Josh felt strange, his arm draped around Jimmy's cold, wet neck, Jimmy's legs accidentally kicking him as he tried to convey Josh toward shore, their bodies shivering together in the cold water. Jimmy and Lenny kept trading off until they reached shore and climbed out on land.

My back was sore from sitting on the wooden plank, and I was getting bored and hot. After popping open a Coke, I reeled in, watching my bobber skip across the lake, planning to check my minnow, but my line was crossed over Grandpa's, and, when I pulled up my hook, I had his line in my hand, too. He glared at me and said, "Watch where you're casting that thing." The way he said "that thing" made it sound more like I had a gaffing hook and I was such a fishing disaster that I might jerk his head off his shoulders with my next cast.

"Anyway," he grunted, "your Uncle Curtis he told me all about that tie-snake. Me and your Uncle Glen, Lucy's husband, and Curtis was always drive over to Muskogee together and go bowling. Glen wore a floppy fishing hat all the time, even at the bowling alley. Now, there's a man could work a lure like nobody's business. Me and him hit every spot of water around here. Couldn't hardly bowl to save his life, though. Curtis always give him a bad time about his bowling. If Glen wasn't with us at the bowling alley, Curtis says you might as well just tell stories because they's no one to laugh at. Long time ago, Curtis says, two men out somewheres hunting together. Camping and hunting, out in the woods. So it gets time to go off to sleep, and the two lay down on opposite sides of the fire and after a while the one of them is sleeping hard but see that other old boy gets hungry, him, and he thinks how much he likes fish real good and how fish fry sound tasty 'bout now. Just then he notices water dripping from the top of the tree a-splashing down on the ground, just falling *ker-plunk* in a puddle from those stripped branches 'cause it's wintertime, no leaves. He waked up his friend who wasn't any too happy about leaving his snooze and says, 'Hey you ain't gonna b'lieve this nohow. Look yonder,' and his friend rubs his eyes. The man who like fish real good says, 'I go up and see what's causing all that commotion.' Up in the top of that tree he found some water and fishes swimming in it up there splashing every whichaways from dashing around.

"That ole boy get a big grin and says, 'How 'bout it, that's what I been wanting,' and throwed him down some of them catfishes to his buddy.

Then he climbed down the tree and cleaned them up and getting ready to dip them in flour and cornmeal and fry them fishes when his friend says, 'There may be something bad wrong 'bout fish found way up in a tree thataway.' That old boy too hungry to worry, and he eats them fish all up so good even clean his teeth with the bones afterwards. His friend won't touch a one of them. So now he's full sure enough but not feeling so hot no mores thinking maybe he kinda overeat too much and he stretched out and said his bones ached little bit. His buddy says, 'Well, I told you they might be no good,' and they both finally go to sleeping on their sides of the fire.

"So this here one who ate the fish woke up in the middle of the night and couldn't b'lieve his eyes and shook his friend real hard and hollering, 'Look here what's the matter with me?' His friend looked and jumped back now seeings how his buddy's legs glued together. 'Well, I told you 'bout that fish. I don't reckon there's nothing we can do,' and he went back off to sleep, that other one. 'Bout the middle of the night he wakes him back up and now his body head down is tail of a snake. Come daybreak, he wakes up his friend one more time and saying to him, 'Look at me now,' and he's completely a snake then, laying there in a big coil.

"So the snake says—he could still talk—'Friend, you gonna have to leave me, but first could you take me over to the water hole?' The snake slithered off into the hole when his friend turned him loose on the bank and that hole commenced to cave in on itself and getting bigger and the water to whirlpool around right fast in the middle. Snake raise up his head out of that rush of water and says, 'Tell my parents and sisters come down here an' visit me.' So his friend brought back to the spot same place all them ones who is kin. They stood on the bank, and the snake showed himself in the middle of the pond. He come up there and crawled out, crawling over the laps of his parents and sisters where they sat on a log next to the bank, him shedding tears while he crawled. He couldn't talk no mores, so he wasn't able to tell them his story. Then he slid in the water, and they went back home."

I had sat down in the gunwale of the boat to rest my back against the bench, keeping one eye on my bobber, the other on Grandpa as he told his story. I had half a dozen questions, and often his stories ended like that, with no explanations. "How could water be in the top of a tree?" I asked him, "and how did the fish get there in the first place? What happened to the snake afterwards?"

Grandpa said, "Hush up, gotta little bite," and readied himself for the next strike. As I wondered if this was the real thing or an avoidance of my pesky curiosity, he jerked his pole back, and it bent over in a wide half-arc while he started steadily working the fish toward the boat.

When they climbed up on the bank, Sammy stood on top, laughing. He had watched the whole thing from shore. "I see the rat didn't drown after all. Hey, Jimmy, I didn't know you liked teaching little girls to swim. Yeah, I seen you lean over and kiss him on the raft. What's the matter, Jimmy? Ashamed of your new girlfriend?"

On solid ground, Jimmy suddenly realized the way he was standing with one arm around Josh's waist, helping him to remain on his feet. He looked down at his arm with revulsion and let go; Josh sagged to his hands and knees in the grass. Jimmy started talking fast. "I just thought I'd dive down and check. I mean he probably can't even swim, what the fuck? I couldn't just let him die." Jimmy spit out his words. "Do you think I liked watching him puke all over himself? I just didn't want to get in trouble. What do you think his folks would say if we left him there? Good thing I dived down when I did." Jimmy kept talking faster, all the while explaining, getting hoarser, looking into Sammy's eyes for some reassurance.

Josh quivered and pulled himself to his feet. His eyes burned from way back, and he snarled, "I didn't need your goddamn help. I almost had that line unwrapped myself. Anyway, I could of stayed down there another couple minutes. I knew how to swim before you were crawling around on the kitchen floor. I could have if I wanted to, goddammit. I was just about to get it untied when you messed me up and I. . . ."

Josh began to weep as the words drifted away from him like smoke. The other boys turned away disgustedly and walked up the bank toward the road, Jimmy the last one to leave. Josh heard their voices, laughing, like the small rasps of a steel file against wood. As they moved up the grassy hill, playing and shoving each other back down, Josh felt himself float out over his own body. He could see his skinny brown frame; it looked no more than an outline, a wisp of smoke that could easily blow away out over the lake. The boys, joking from the hillside, sounded like their voices came from deep within the belly of a cave where words dripped down red-streaked walls and echoed through caverns full of meanings he could not grasp. Confusion washed over him.

He watched Sammy and Lenny walking down the road that led home. Jimmy paused for an instant and turned back toward the lake. He approached slowly, and he stood off from Josh, looking down at him from the top of the bank. He waited until Sammy and Lenny were out of earshot. He stared at his feet as he spoke. "You know the guys. They're just playing around."

Josh did not reply. The waves patted the shore in rhythmic claps. "Well, you know how it is around them, don't you?" Jimmy coughed and lit a cigarette. He waited for Josh to say something. He looked out toward the raft. "I didn't really mean it. I just didn't want them to think, well, you know how they tease you if they think you like someone too much."

Josh couldn't find the right words for his rage. He felt all the words flaming up before his eyes and burning away like stubble before he could use them. In church he had heard Jesus's words to the centurion: Speak the Word and you shall be healed. He no longer believed. He wished he could pick up words like stones, rub them to make them smooth and polished, and put them in his pocket to save and use during moments like this one. He longed for the comfort of those stones. He wished he had collected all kinds of them—agate streaked with red lightning, hard quartz pounded into indissoluble rage, blood-red hematite formed around secrets, yellow amaranth rained down by tears. He would put all the rocks in his mouth and find his voice in their swirled streaks of sky, fire, water. But there were no such rocks and none of them contained secret messages and there was nobody to send them to even if they had.

Jimmy snuffed out his cigarette on a broken willow trunk, flicking the stub into the grass. "Well, I guess I'll be seeing you around," he said. He turned and walked off toward the road.

"Yeah, I guess," Josh said.

Lord of the losers that summer, I lived inside my imagination and often felt myself floating away, as others talked, into my private world of dreams. But not when Grandpa launched into his stories, which demanded some kind of listening akin to physical participation, and he cast his voice in such a way that drew you into the presences his words created. Bored on the boat with no place to go, bored with staring at my bobber ride up one hill of waves and down the slippery slope of another, bored with trying to will a fish into hunger for my minnow or dangling night crawler, Grandpa's stories were a welcome, if strange, respite. And if I wasn't fishing with him, my grandma would send me over to my cousins to "play with boys your own age instead of being locked up in that room with those books of yours."

Grandpa strung his bass on the stringer, running the clasp through its mouth and gill slit and closing it, then tossing the chain in the water, the only catch of the day. Maybe that very fish had been violently jerked out of its underwater home, from the barn or farmhouse my grandparents used to live in before the lake covered up their former residence. He settled back into the bench, and I saw his eyelids flutter and his head start to nod off. I couldn't believe it; even he was bored with fishing. Afraid that he might fall over, I said, loud enough to rouse him, yet tentatively, knowing how much a pain in the ass I was on fishing trips, "Hey, wake up."

"Ain't asleep," he muttered, and when he surfaced from his nap, he came up in the middle of another story as if he'd never stopped talking. He tied a bass plug onto his line while he spoke.

"A *micco* one time he send his son out with a message for another chief. Sent him out with that message in a clay pot so the chief would recognize him. His son stopped to play with some boys—he was carrying that clay pot you know—who were throwing stones into the water. Pitching and throwing. Making them rocks skip. Chief's son wanting to show off a little bit maybe he can do it better than all them other ones, so he throwed that vessel on the water, but it sank. Like this here."

Grandpa laid down his pole for a second and tossed an imaginary pot in an easy underhanded curve out into the lake. "That boy 'fraid to go to the neighbor chief without his father's message, more 'fraid to go back home and tell his father he lost him his pot. He jumped into that stream and got to the place where it sunk and dove down under there. His playmates waited a long time round that creek for him to come back up but never did. They went back home and told everyone he died.

"Underneath that murky water tie-snake grabbed a-holt of him and drug him off to a cave where he lived. Inside, tie-snake says, 'See that platform over yonder? Get up on there, you.' Up on the platform was the king of the tie-snakes." Grandpa dropped his voice and sounded commanding when he imitated the tie-snake ordering the chief's son.

"The boy didn't like too good what he saw; that platform was a heap of crawling snakes. Oh, they was just crawling around. Slithering around. Sliding around. Weaving in and out of each other. And that king sitting big up on a ledge right over there on that platform.

"Well, this boy walked up there anyway trying to not let on how scared he was. Plumb frightened. He lifted his foot to get up on the platform, but, as he did, it just rose up higher. He tried again, same thing. And a third time. That tie-snake said again, 'Get up yonder, boy,' and on the fourth try he got up there. King invited him come sit down on that ledge next to him. 'Better than them wiggling snakes all round my feet,' the boy thinks. King says, 'Over yonder is a feather; it's yours,' pointing to a cluster of red tail feathers from a hawk. That boy went over and reached out and every time his fingers went to grabbing those feathers they disappeared. But on the fourth try he got it and held to it.

"He goes back over to tie-snake who says, 'That knife over yonder is yours.' Same thing again. It rose up on its own every time the chief's son raise up his hand. On the fourth time it didn't go nowheres, and he laid holt of it. The king said the boy could go back home after four days. King says, 'If your father asks where you been gone, say, I know what I know, but no matter what don't tell him what you know. When your father needs my help, walk toward the east and bow four times to the rising sun, and I will be there to help him.'

"Tie-snake took the boy back after four days, up to the surface where he first dived under and put the lost vessel back in his hands. The boy swam to the bank and went home to his father who was right happy to see him seeings how he thought he was dead.

"Boy told his father about tie-snake king and his offer to help, but he didn't tell his father what he knew. His father heard about enemies planning an attack, and he sent his boy off to get help. The chief's son put the feathered plume on his head, grabbed up his knife, headed towards the east. He bowed four times before the sunrise, and there stood tie-snake king in front of him.

"'What do you need?' he asked.

"'My father needs your help,' the boy answered.

"'Don't worry none,' tie-snake told him. 'They will attack but nobody get hurt. Go back and tell him I'll make it all right.'

"The boy went back and delivered the message. The enemy came and attacked the town but no one got hurt. It came nighttime, and there were their enemies on the edge of the village all caught up in a tangled mess of snakes."

Grandpa was pulling up the coffee-can cement anchor since it was starting to get dark out. Crickets were chirruping on shore, and fireflies flitted here and there over the water. I burned to know the boy's secret, what he withheld from his father, what lay buried beneath the shadowy water, but already Grandpa was set on rowing, rowing toward shore.

Michael Koby

Santa Claus, Indiana

I think I remember her, all bucktoothed and stringy hair, she looked more like a babysitter than a mom, buying diapers down at the Piggly Wiggly all pigtails and glitter nail polish. She was sixteen years old when I popped out. She lived with her mamma. I don't know much about my daddy. My grandma was French and real old-fashioned. I was around two or three years when the fire broke out. Ma woke up to smoke. She rushed round cursing to herself, pillow feathers a-flying as she gathered up this and that. I wasn't panicky, I liked the way she hurried round like a slaughter chicken. She got me out quick, but didn't have enough time to save her own ma. From all accounts, she went crazy after that. Sometimes I think I remember that fire. I wake up with images of a burning bed and a body melting into the mattress springs. Mamma and me had nowhere to go. She gave me up. I was given to the people that raised me in a blanket with fancy blue and pink roses embroidered on the edge. Right away, my new ma called me something different, and I play-pretended I was somebody she could like. Truth is I pretty much forgot my real name. She looked more like my ma than the other one ever did, all blond and blue-eyed, like somebody on the television. She said I had been named after Michael Landon, that he was the biggest hunk this side of the Dixie border. People called me Michael, Mike, Mikey (like the cereal kid who liked everything), Mickey Mouse, even Sunshine, but nobody ever called me P.J. again.

In second grade Mamma stood in front of the T.V. as I tried watching Lon Chaney Jr. creep through the black-and-white fog as a werewolf, her legs and miniskirt blocking out the picture's center. I knew something was about to happen 'cause she never bothered me when I was watching my favorite movie; she knew how bad I wanted to be a monster. Interrupting my study, she crouched down, teary-eyed and running blue mascara.

She told me what I already figured, that she and my daddy weren't my real family. I knew I was too damn bright to be related to these people; they were always busy ignoring how the sun spilled on the carpet at one o'clock or how the damned dog snarled when you'd wink at it. I swallowed hard, waiting dry-mouthed for this mother person to tell me the truth I knew already, that I wasn't a Dutchman, but some sort of monster not like her at all. I had noticed how my hair was turning color and my eyes too. I didn't really look like either of um no more. Of course I wasn't related to um; they were pure blond and good.

She crouched down all frightened like, smiling one of those smiles that you don't want to see in the dark.

"Your mamma was young. Your gramma's house burnt down and she had nobody. She ain't your mommy; I'm your mommy 'cause I wanted you so bad. I chose you; she birthed you is all. They were poor anyway, at least now you got a swimmin' pool."

A sudden rush crept up my toes and into my tummy, something between that tingling ya feel before you pee and the numbness of sticking your hand in the icebox. I stared right in her eyes, sucking in the little spit behind my bottom teeth so I wouldn't lisp like a sissy.

"Mamma, what was my real name, the one that lady gave me, the one she called me?"

Straight to my face, her cheeks streaked blue, makeup spiders running from her eyes, like that nice Jesus lady on Sunday morning T.V., always crying 'bout nothing. She didn't blink, stutter, or swear.

"Michael. Your name has always been Michael."

Laura M. Furlan

Aunt Lucy

You look just like her, he told me, in the photograph I'd just sent. I had never met my Aunt Lucy, just as I still had not met my father. Sometimes I talk to him on the phone.

Tell me about her, I say to him, more than once, conscious of my accent, not southern, not from Mississippi. I slip into his drawl sometimes, the sounds so natural to my ear. I imagine Lucy must have spoken this way.

I grew up not looking like anyone, so I cannot picture Lucy, this older version of me. She must have had my blue eyes, my clefted chin. I wonder if her hair became darker when she reached my age.

She only comes around for money, he says, not long before she dies. She drank and drifted. It would have been hard to track her down. Maybe he'll send me a photo one day, then I'll see the resemblance. She was an Indian, he says, and I wonder what he means.

D. M. O'Brien

Living Memory

We are the Lost Generation
third in line
in schools now closed.

We mirror forced reflections
skin itching
feeling tight;
scarred by sacred switches
leaving marks
sinking into muscle
scraping bone
contaminating the marrow.

We are daughters and sons
exchanging roles and intermixing
and being punished—
slashed with words and hands
raped by our own families
recycling the hurts.

We are the
Saving Seventh Generation
ready to change the world.

We are neotraditional
dancing and singing

with large drums—
jingle dressing
and high flying bustles.

We are waking healers
talking old words
now translated
into adopted Mother tongues
and spoken from dreams
in a language we can't speak—
except in our blood.

We are the lost memories
in a group consciousness
trying desperately
to remember a past
that glorified our lives
our sexuality
our prize.

William Raymond Taylor

Gathering of Nations

At Gathering of Nations we ate Indian tacos and drank coffees
Served us by a kid wearing a "Frybread Power" t-shirt,
Walked the promenade of the basketball arena, touched
Porcupine quill medicine wheels made for non-believers and
    bowed
In respect at their craftsmanship. From the stands I squinted
Through an old prescription at the dancers far below, women
Decked out in tin cones and shawls, fringe swaying with the drum
Then men's fancy and my heart ached;
I felt the initial drum beats, whole body tensed for the leap into song
From first step to honor beats, breath pant
Drum sticks that hit the rim of the drum, drum silenced, the singers
    left
To carry the rhythm of the song, still dancing
With porcupine roach flexing, feathers rocking, U-shaped bustles
Like living flames of green and blue amongst the neon-orange, yellow
    and red,
Bells strapped under knees, shout to rafters, turn and see a dancer
Disqualified after a feather dropped from his shoulder and spiraled to
    the floor;
Still in the Circle, but out of the competition. I once sang with a
    Blackfoot man
Loved his son, and when my brother stopped dancing, certain

He was too light-skinned to ever be accepted
I stopped as well, but I kept the tapes: Porcupine Singers, Grass
    Dance songs
So when heavy-hearted and depressed, I reach for powwow music
And know my place in the Circle.

Janice Gould

Indian Mascot, 1959

Now begins the festival and rivalry of late fall,
the weird debauch and daring debacle
of frat-boy parties as students parade foggy streets in mock
processions, bearing on shoulders scrawny effigies of dead
defeated Indians cut from trees, where,
in the twilight, they had earlier been hung.

"Just dummies," laughs our dad, "Red Indians hung
or burned—it's only in jest." Every fall
brings the Big Game against Stanford, where
young scholars let off steam before the debacle
they may face of failed exams. "You're dead
wrong," he says to Mom, "They don't mock

real, live Indians." Around U.C. campus mock
lynchings go on. Beneath porches we see hung
the scarecrow Natives with fake long braids, dead
from the merry-making. On Bancroft Way one has fallen
indecorously to a lawn, a symbol of the debacle
that happened three generations ago in California's hills, where

Native peoples were strung up. (A way of having fun? Where
did they go, those Indian ghosts?) "Their kids perform mock
war dances, whooping, reenacting scenes of a debacle
white folks let loose," chides Mom. "Meanwhile we hang

portraits of presidents on school walls and never let fall
the old red, white, and blue. My dear brother is dead

because he fought in a white man's war. How many dead
Indians do they need to feel okay? This whole thing wears
on my soul." In the dark car we go silent, and the fall
night gets chillier. In yards, blazing bonfires mock
the stars that glow palely somewhere above. A thin moon hangs
over the tule fogs. I've never heard the word "debacle"

before and wonder what it means. "What's a debacle,
Mom?" I ask. "Oh, honey, it's a terrible and deadly
collapse. Complete ruin." I've noticed how the hung
Indians have their heads slumped forward. They wear
old clothes, headbands with feathers, face paint, moc-
casins instead of boots. Little do we know this fall

living Indians at Feather Falls
leave tobacco to mark that, indeed,
we're still here, lungs full of indigenous air.

Malea Powell

real Indians

the real indian leans against
the counter at the white castle just off I-65 two miles south of the pow-
wow grounds alongside wapaashiiki, the wabash river whose sycamored
banks and water-pitted caves whisper the voices of my elders
but we are here now, not there,
and here is next in line staring out at the parking lot piece-quilted with
trucks and cars and campers, the last space surprised by that listing Win-
nebago, y'know, that Ho-Chunk guy who still smells like the last lonely
piece of frybread those Santa Clara guys finally got rid of halfway through
the last giveaway

or maybe
here isn't here at all, but there, at the drive-thru ordering a PakASak of
30 with cheese plus some chicken rings and onion petals to go, to keep
us company on that long drive across I-80—Lake Michigan, the Illinois,
the Mississippi, the Iowa, the Missouri, the Platte, all those rivers, all those
miles of hiway on fire, the land twisted black like winter wind, the sky a
smear of pink cotton candy stuffed into the greedy mouth of a white man
whose teeth grind us into the plains

or maybe
what I hear is a mourning song, one that sounds exactly like an orange
tiger cat crying, trying to claw her way out of her lavender-plastic, seat-
belted cage, you know, that song I sing every time we get too far away from

Miami land and Meier stores and French & Indian war monuments and
A & W rootbeer stands open only in the summer and the sound of the
Twigh Twee singers as they warm up before first grand entry and the way
that white castles
>   **never**
>   taste
>   when you buy them frozen, no peeling away the warm gooey bun from
the steamed meat center to add hot mustard and pickles before you eat
them in three bites and twelve bites later are too drunk with grease to eat
anymore

or maybe
>   what I hear when i'm here is the sound of us not dying or disappearing,
just eating and talking and laughing and driving,
>   remembering who we are

Deborah Miranda

Coyote Takes a Trip

Standing in the cold, sand-swept Venice Beach parking lot watching his clothing scatter in the four directions, Coyote decided to head for New Mexico, catch up with his brother, and leave his broken heart behind.

He'd been living on Venice Beach for a long time; he liked the ocean with its tall jade winter waves and generous people who camped in the parking lot. Something about their vehicles—old school buses, pickup trucks with hand-made campers, station wagons from the 1970s equipped with curtains and propane stoves—felt like home. Coyote was always welcome to add a paw print or play with bright paints, contribute his own unique touch to the vivid vehicle decor. And no one objected to his new favorite signature, a bumper sticker of two naked women kissing, emblazoned FUCK CENSORSHIP.

"I have substantial evidence that those Indian men who, both here [Santa Barbara] and farther inland, are observed in the dress, clothing, and character of women – there being two or three such in each village – pass as sodomites by profession (it being confirmed that all these Indians are much addicted to this abominable vice) and permit the heathen to practice the execrable, unnatural abuse of their bodies. They are called joyas [jewels], and are held in great esteem." (Pedro Fages, soldier, 1775)

On Venice Beach, even in the winter Coyote could get cheap pizza by the slice at a kiosk that also sold Pall Malls and condoms, find regular guys always up for a good game of go or checkers, or soak up an afternoon's entertainment from a wandering minstrel with a sexy 3-string guitar and cheerfully resigned dog. Not to mention the sweet crazy woman with sleeping bags in the back of her van just waiting for Coyote to heat them—and her—up.

But this one winter, the rain just didn't let up. The sand never dried out, the paint bled off his best graffiti, and the sleeping bags felt damp and gritty. Heavy squalls blew in off the Pacific day after day, the checker players hunched grouchily under the few covered shelters arguing about whose turn it was to score some hot coffee, and even the cement walkway between Venice Beach and the Santa Monica Pier seemed sodden. *Must be friggin' global warming,* Coyote muttered to himself, wringing out the only pair of socks he owned (who needed more than one pair of socks in Southern California?)—*world's goin' ta hell these days.*

Yeah, Coyote figured maybe he'd take a road trip to see his brother in the drier climes of New Mexico, where it might be colder, but at least a guy could stand outside for a smoke without wearing a plastic garbage bag. Seemed like his sweet crazy woman wasn't so sweet anymore. Maybe more crazy than sweet, eh? Why else would she move her van while he was out cruising—er, walking, the beach? He'd come back from a little hot chocolate sipping under the pier to find his rickety suitcase teetering, lonely and frayed, in an empty parking space.

"Gah!" Coyote surveyed his wardrobe of obscene T-shirts and gangsta pants scattered amongst the scraggly pigeons and seagulls, grabbed a few handfuls (time was, he wouldn't be caught dead with baggage, but the economy wasn't what it used to be). He tucked the soggy mess into the rickety rolling suitcase that served as pack mule and safety deposit box, shook the sand out of his fur, hitched up his low-riding green canvas pants, and slouched up the hill to catch a #1 Santa Monica Big Blue Bus to Westwood. From there he could catch a shuttle to LAX, where he had relatives who worked in baggage.

Maybe one of them could box him up and put him on a nonstop to ABQ. Anything would be better than this soggy gray sponge of a beach!

Trudging past the bright but mostly empty tattoo shops, massage parlors, and taquerias in Venice, Coyote wondered how his life had taken such a tragic turn.

He'd lost his mojo, that's what it was—lost his touch, lost his way, lost his magic. It must be these SoCal women he'd been hanging with. They just sucked the life right out of a guy, and not in a good way. Made him feel every one of his immemorial years old. Geez, they wanted you to bring home groceries!

As if that's what Coyote does.

Groceries? Gah. What woman in her right mind would waste her Coyote on groceries?

Yeah, he'd never had any trouble getting fed or otherwise taken care of—until this winter. But something—maybe the endless rain—was diluting his powers.

My prowess! thought Coyote, bumping his old green suitcase up and over curbs and around puddles. *Dude, where's my prowess? I can't even hold my tail up anymore, let alone my pecker.*

The shoulders of his jean jacket slumped, excess inches of pants sloshing in the rain; Coyote stood at the bus stop with water dripping off his snout and didn't even have the heart to flick his ears.

Oh well. At least the bus was pulling up, he had 75 cents for the ride, and there was his brother's wife's cooking in the near future. Just thinking about a big round bowl of Macaria's smoldering beans topped with diced peppers and some hunks of goat cheese cheered Coyote up a little bit. And oh, Macaria's homemade corn tortillas!

He perked up enough to let three old ladies get on the bus ahead of him.

Of course that meant the three old ladies took the last three seats on the bus, the row right up front under the sign that said in English and Spanish, "Please give up these seats for elderly and handicapped patrons." On the opposite wall of the bus, behind the driver, were more seats, but they'd been folded up earlier for a wheelchair and never restored.

Coyote lurched awkwardly trying to pull the seats down without losing his balance on the already-moving bus, but he couldn't find just the right button or switch. *Story of my life,* he growled. Finally he just threw his suitcase down on the floor and plopped right on it. He smiled up innocently at the three old ladies—one black, one *India*, one Korean—as he perched at their feet.

Buncha dried-up old viejas. What's so funny?

Crouching on his suitcase at eye level with three old women's knobby knees, his cold feet throbbing and wet pants clinging to his cold calves, Coyote made a strange discovery. It was something he'd never noticed before: All three of these broads had perfectly dry pant hems. Of course that meant that when they sat down their high-waters rose practically to their knees, but he had to admit, it also meant they didn't suffer from water wicking up the fabric and freezing them to death, either.

Interesting, Coyote thought, but distinctly un-cool.

And in the gap between the saggy tops of their white tube socks and the bottom of their nylon stretch-waist pants, strips of even less attractive bare, hairy skin gaped.

Ay!

Well, hairy on four of the six legs—at least the indigenous woman, the one in the middle, seemed relatively smooth-skinned. . . .

Coyote sniffed.

She used lotion, too, or maybe just a nice laundry detergent. Fresh. Lilacs, maybe, or could it be lavender? Gee, it'd been so long since he'd been with a woman who actually did her laundry with something besides public restroom pump soap.

Coyote tilted his head so he could get a look at that middle woman's hands grasping the curved dark top of her wooden cane. He didn't want to seem obvious.

Ah, yes. A modest but tasteful home-manicure. Nails not long enough to do a guy damage, but grown out a bit, filed, polished with clear stuff, and clean. No wedding band, he noticed, but a nice silver signet ring on the left pinky, turquoise stone, probably a high school sweetheart's old token. Cinnamon-colored skin, weather-worn but not too wrinkly, hard-working hands, sturdy hands with calluses and a few old scars across the back, a scattering of well-deserved age spots.

She would never have been a beauty, Coyote admitted, but with those hands, she surely could have made a man happy.

She even had a cloth shopping bag sticking out of her coat pocket; obviously, off to the grocery store. Senior Tuesday at Von's, he remembered. Important day for those beach dwellers on a budget.

He risked a quick glance up at her face as she shifted to let someone squeeze toward the exit. She knew how to use makeup, that was certain; a little foundation, some blue eye-shadow but not too much, and a discreet but feminine coral pink lipstick. A bit heavy on the rouge, perhaps, but then again, maybe that extra tinge was from the effort of hoofing it up to the bus stop in the rain. Firm chin, a good nose with some arch to it; not ashamed of her strength, he decided. Her hair, mostly silver with black streaks, pulled back into a tight braid, protected from the elements by one of those plastic baggie-things old women always carry in their purses.

Suave, in a sweet way.

She'd tied a silky blue scarf, just the right color to set off her eye-shadow, at her throat. Coyote would've liked a better look at her neck, but as it was, he was surprised to find that one old woman could hold his attention this long.

Shi-i-i-t. What was he thinking? He was on his way outta here, not the best time to be ogling a woman. Disgruntled and hungry, he looked out the wide front windows at the rain and resisted the awful thought that he was inside a mobile aquarium. Okay, he thought: I'm on the road, heading toward a whole plate of Macaria's enchiladas. . . .

The longer he sat on his rickety old suitcase on the floor of the bus, the better Coyote felt about his decision. It was time to clear out of L.A. Venice Beach in the winter was no place for an unappreciated Coyote like him! He needed to be where stories were told, hot food dished up, and a woman was only wet when he made her that way himself. Yeah. Albuquerque for sure, hit some bars with his brother, a few excursions to the Pueblos. Didn't he have an old girlfriend at Zuni?

"When the missionaries first arrived in this region [San Diego], they found men dressed as women and performing women's duties, who were kept for unnatural purposes. From their youth up they were treated, instructed, and used as females, and were even frequently publicly married to the chiefs or great men . . . Being more robust than the women, they were better able to perform the arduous duties required of the wife, and for this reason, they were often selected by the chiefs and others, and on the day of the wedding a grand feast was given." (Fr. Geronimo Boscana, 1846)

Lost in his dreams of glory, culinary and otherwise, Coyote damn near missed his stop.

Wait! he yelped, leaping up to snag the yellow pull-cord and bending down just as rapidly to grab the worn handle of his rickety suitcase. *Wait for me!*

Scrabbling, Coyote had an odd, hobbled sensation, like a horse, unable to move more than a few increments in any direction no matter how hard he tried. And what was that cold breeze at his back—or rather, his backside?

Just as he straightened fully, suitcase firmly grasped in his left hand, Coyote's very baggy pants, held up by a dirty-white piece of rope, suddenly became a lot baggier.

Oops.

Not only was his butt hanging out for all the world to see, but so was his pride and joy, and wouldn't you know it, right at eye level with the old *Indita* who'd been ignoring him the whole ride.

There was something about her expression that he couldn't quite figure out, but it reminded him of his brother's face when they'd hit the jackpot in Vegas one time.

An involuntary guffaw escaped Coyote's mouth as he grabbed the front of his pants and yanked up, clung desperately to the handle of his suitcase, and tried to spontaneously sprout another hand as the bus driver went from 30 mph to nothing, screeching to a halt. Barreling forward, Coyote blew right past the driver, bounced off the dashboard down the steps, landed breathless and barely clothed at the foot of a gently dripping palm tree.

He looked up at the bus windows to see three pairs of eyes staring back.

The black woman's face was mapped with new laugh lines Coyote knew he had just personally inscribed.

The Korean grandma's eyes glittered with outrage, her lips moving with words he was glad he could only imagine.

But the old Indian lady—could it be—was he just imagining it, or— well, was she giving him the *eye*?

Admiring his prowess? Almost applauding what she'd witnessed for one brief sweet second?

Coyote felt it then: his mojo.

Like an illegal firecracker smuggled off the rez, like a long drink out of a fresh bottle of tequila, it was coming back to him, streaming into him, filling him with a terrible joy: That was no little old lady. The qualities that had so intrigued Coyote, that mix of strength and serene femininity . . . that old lady was a glammed-up—*and impressed*—old man.

The bus squealed outta there, the driver blasting into traffic, and Coyote found himself with a suitcase in one hand, his family jewels in the other, and a confused but very happy mojo.

He stared after the bus, unconsciously licking his chops.

Not exactly a man. What was that old word?

Joto?

No, older than that, and sweeter.

Joya? Jewel of the People?

Nope, still Spanish, and just thinking it conjured up vile images of humiliation before loved ones, being stripped naked, mastiffs set loose, flesh and souls mutilated. *No, we had our own words before the padres and soldados de cuero*, Coyote thought; it was coming back to him now, how many beautiful words, each tribe creating a title as unique as the being it described.

Standing on the sidewalk, Coyote rolled his slippery pink tongue around in his mouth as if he could rattle the lost names out from between his teeth somewhere. One word in particular, something he'd learned long ago on a warm beach, whispered by a Ventureño with sparkling eyes and a ticklish belly . . . a word that meant honor, medicine, truth . . . then his mouth remembered, and Coyote cried the Chumash word aloud:

'aqi!

He looked down the street toward the airport shuttle stop.

Then back down Westwood toward Santa Monica Boulevard, and Venice Beach.

S/he must live down there. He was sure he'd seen hir around. Yeah, s/he sat off to the side during checkers matches and read books, sometimes brought a bag of cookies from the Hostess discount bakery to share. Always had a warm chuckle when Coyote threw up his arms in triumph, or a soft "Awww . . . " and a *click* of tongue in sympathy when Coyote slumped in defeat.

What name did the *'aqi* go by? Dolores? Estéfana?

Juanita.

It was *really* cold in ABQ this time of year, Coyote remembered. Ice, even.

Slowly Coyote pulled up his baggies and reknotted the ratty rope around his waist. He replayed that swift glance of pleasure from Juanita, his thrilling moment of chaotic revelation, his tail waving and erect.

Then, without waiting for the light to change, he pulled out the extended handle of his rickety rolling suitcase and hauled it across the street, where the Big Blue Bus #1 headed down to Venice for a mere 75 cents.

A *cheap trip*, Coyote smiled amidst a chorus of honks from a Prius, a Mercedes, and a shiny yellow Hummer, accented by well-honed expletives from their drivers. He didn't mind. Now he knew where his mojo had gone, and he was gonna be there waiting when it came back this afternoon.

Hell, he might even help carry the groceries.

"The priests [at Mission Santa Clara] were advised that two pagans had gone into one of the houses of the neophytes, one in his natural raiment, the other dressed as a woman. Such a person [was] called a joya. Immediately the missionary, with the corporal and a soldier, went to the house to see what they were looking for, and they found the two in an unspeakably sinful act. They punished them, although not so much as deserved. The priest tried to present to them the enormity of their deed. The pagan replied that that joya was his wife." (Fr. Francisco Palou, 1777)

Louis Esmé Cruz

Birth Song for Muin, in Red

In a room with an open window there is a tiny, red rocking chair from the old days. It is empty and motionless beside the window and a cool, late autumn breeze stirs the dust that's collected there. It belongs to a young girl, and with no immediate family to look after her, she sets out for other sanctuaries. It has been a while but she is coming back for this rocking chair now, though you may not recognize her from when she sat in it before, and she will barely recognize it herself because it has been just that long. The young girl will have to rock very slowly before she will even remember a time when she knew she was this alone.

The young girl has no immediate family and sometimes goes without food or sleeps in the bushes when there isn't a relative to provide these things. She learns to gather wild berries, learning through trial and error the ones that don't make her sick.

While out searching for food in the forest one day, the young girl catches a glimpse of something sparkly out of the corner of her eye. Turning she sees a group of bears moving on an island of few trees, toward her. Between each tree, banners declare their power: [Remembearing Our Ancestors], [Unbearable Beauties for Sovereign Erotics], [Breed Bears Do It Both Ways]. Fabulously painted poles and platforms frame daring, gender-bent performance. Succulent streamers and flamboyant feathers sharpen Girl's focus toward a familiar yet curious existence. Looking back toward the pre-fab houses behind her, the young girl shudders boredom from her shoulders. Eyes back to the joyous bears, she moves forward from this precipice. Now beside the rolling island of joy, the young girl puts her arms out to the dancing bears who reach back and pull her solid, young body into their fold.

Home though not home, she makes familiar her surroundings. Respectful of her new friends, Girl delights in furry legs wrapped in fishnet; ruby-studded heels; faux-fur and pleather vests; form-fitting turquoise Y-front ginchies; harnesses that grip generous packages; perfect, pink tutus; dark, grey pinstripe suits with gold pocket watches; raunchy motorcycle boots; butch haircuts and tough tattoos; elongated bird nails; tiny, pointed moustaches; beards of ample girth; along with unicycles, tricycles, wheelchairs, canes, and crutches.

This vision of beauty fills her belly with an ache of longing. The young girl's body stirs—a clawing, twisting mass of undulating excitement. With this new sensation growing into an almost unbearable feeling, the young girl cultivates boy skin for protection and strength. The slight fuzz on her face, chest, and arms thickens, as her delicate toes grow wider and hairy.

The island floats further into the forest. Upon reaching this strange, new place, the young girl with this new boy skin is introduced to the most beautiful woman she has ever seen. She puts her tiny hand into Muini'skw's (Bear-woman's) giant paw, feeling the rough-hewn skin as a welcoming embrace. This walloping mama bear is voluptuous with glittering claws and sizable teeth, as handsome as she is rocketing in breast.

Muini'skw looms large above the young girl in boy skin, a situation made more striking by the studded stilettos she insists on wearing while performing her paternal duties. Muini'skw lowers herself down upon a plinth of passionate pink pillows, gesturing for the young girl in boy skin to take a seat in the folds of her furry lap. She prances forward, climbing gaily into Muini'skw's delicious lap.

This world of thickset bears is enticing and she never wants to leave. To return to the world she lived in before, where no one seemed to care whether she lived or died, would crumple the heart she is learning to palpate with her own delicate fist. Her desire to live with the bears is just fine for them, as they enjoy her pleasant company as much as her flair for fine texture. She realizes that she, too, is a bear and that this is her family—more than anyone else has ever been. While contemplating her blessings, the young girl with boy skin understands that given her propensity for masculine glamour, she is as much boy as she is girl. There is only one thing to do: Seek out Muini'skw to find insight into her situation.

The young girl with boy skin and thickening hair cautiously approaches Muini'skw in her wigwam; Muini'skw is reading the latest issue of *Fuzzy-wuzzy*, a popular gossip magazine. Beginning slowly, she shares her feelings with the mama bear, recognizing that her difficulty in forming these words is in part due to the fact that she is carving out her own path. Living with the bears, she knows she is a human girl. Being raised as a human girl, she knows she is also a bear boy. That she is a bear and a boy is no surprise to her, but without the right words to refer to herself, she feels more different now than she did when she was without close human family.

Now, Muini'skw is a glamourous diva who has been around the camp a few times in her stilettos. In her earlier days before she had baby bears of her own, she was known to hang with many different kinds of creatures, so this wasn't the first time she had come across a young one with this dilemma. Muini'skw, being the kind lady she is, gives the child a name to help her hold space in the world: Muinji'j, Bear-boy.

One day while Muinji'j is out with her bear brothers having a gay ole time at the edge of the forest, the periphery of the city, an old friend of Muinji'j's notices them. The old friend was out gathering cranberries and foxberries when his eye catches the familiar movements of a young girl with boy skin and thickening hair behaving like and socializing with bears. Excited to see the girl whose extended family thought her long gone, strange-behaving though she was, the old friend ran home to tell everyone what he had seen.

Back in the forest, Muini'skw wakes from a cinematic sleep showing her the arrival of the young boy with bear skin's human family and the imminent departure of Muinji'j. During the time after his arrival in the forest, when they created many beautiful things together, it had occurred to Muini'skw that Muinji'j might want or need to return to his birth family some day. She hoped that this would not happen for a long time. Now that this day has come, Muini'skw wails with sorrow, her wide face buried in soft pillows. She calls for Muinji'j from this sad heap to share with him her vision. He is angry and confused. Muinji'j claws at her to please, let him stay with the bears because his body still holds memory of the irritating loneliness he felt as a fabulously flamboyant human lost in a tragic tirade of taupe tapestries. Sobbing, Muini'skw holds her growing, furry boy firmly to her magnificent girth. Her giant breasts soaked with his longing, Muini'skw asks Muinji'j to accept responsibility for his unique ability to see the soft space between women and men, bears and humans.

Reluctant, though willing to respect her wishes, Muinji'j pulls back from his tiny diva moment. Muini'skw asks him to carry in every moment all the wonderful things he has learned about bear fabulosity. This was important for humans to understand bears. Knowing this, Muini'skw wanted to bring about more respectful interactions between their families. Some time ago the humans and bears experienced each other in less than loving ways. During this era, everything simplified, forcing relations between mixed lovers, friends, comrades, and even blood-relatives to pick only one side from which to see the world. She also asked that he remember the land between his homes, the pathways between them, so that he could return to her as often as possible. She assured him that her enormous breasts would be there whenever he needed and her aureate arms ready to embrace him with love. Muinji'j, with his different ways of knowing and support from those who also desire peace, takes responsibility to help transform this suffering, moving away from Muini'skw's embrace toward his uncertain future.

Returning to his den, Muinji'j gathers the few belongings he will need on his travels and in his new/old home. Each of the gifts carries with it medicines to protect, nurture, suture, and remind him of everything he has learned and continues to learn. He makes his way around the circle of bears coming in from all parts of the forest to send him off with blessings, breathing in their love/cedar. Hummingbird, Dragonfly, and Raven rhyme, scratch, and throw down beats for his departure. Turning to leave, Muinji'j gathers his spirit in to himself. He steps out.

Slipping through forest, over mountain, treading through grass, across plain, over fresh lake, around bog, scaling more mountain, then salty water and finally craggy rock, Muinji'j feels his heartbeat growing louder as he nears home. He pauses to take a drink from the rumbling river, feeling the prayer it sings to his internal estuaries, urging him further.

Noticing subtle variation in bark texture and colour, leaves lean in greens new and old to his eyes, shapes of stones sharpen and harden edges under foot—Muinji'j looks inside for the first time, as a man coming to the edge of a precipice. No longer a youth, he remembers his early years with tenderness. No longer Girl, he recognizes his maturity and strength. No longer human, nor simply bear, he acknowledges his human-bear-ness—all of this alive in the whole of his complicated body. In these moments of integrating while moving toward his land and people, Muinji'j receives the gift of wholeness. Wampum weaves his dignified heart.

Years later, Muinji'j sits in his old, red rocking chair and as he does this, calf muscles twitch, feet bones crack into place. Rolling pressure from heel to toe, then back to heel, he picks up the dance that began a long time ago. He remembers rolling soil and sand with these claws, crunching leaves beneath them, and pinching his older bear-brothers between their boney structures.

His hair is long now. Sometimes he takes the time to fold the wiry strands into braids.

Looking down at his aged body he has carried all this time, he sees a softened man in blue jean overalls—he is the same but different. His arms are those of a bear's and even his large hands claw that old, red rocking chair.

Everything has shifted around him, showing that some time has passed. Inside his mind, he is still that sharp, little girl with eyes seeing everything. All these memories recognize Muinji'j, showing him the path that lost him and the love that brought him back. (Whitehead 26–30)

Whitehead, Ruth Holmes. "Traditional Story: The Boy Who Visited Muini'skw." In *The Mi'kmaq Anthology*. Nova Scotia: Pottersfield Press, 1997. RHW notes: Retold from stories collected by Silas Rand ("A Child Nourished by a Bear," and a variant on the same, 1894: 259–261); from Wallis and Wallis ("A Boy Who Lived with the Bears," 1955: 431); and from Elsie Clews Parsons ("The [Bear] Ancestor of the Sylliboy Family," 1925: 96–97).

Qwo-Li Driskill

Chantway for F.C.

I

From the heavy debris of loss
we emerge
with giveaways of yellow and white corn
to anoint the tip of your tongue
feast on the memory of your first laughter
sing an honor song
to the slow heartbeat
of your final breaths

Together we emerge
voices strained and weary from wailing

We emerge in beauty
You will be our song

II

Grief pulls me
down canyon walls

                              There I wander

to search for imprints
your hands left in dust

                              There I wander

71

Hold up hot fierce
blueness of Colorado sky

> *There I wander*

Listen for your breath
caught in branches

> *There I wander*

Hunger for your voice
in a piñon jay's throat

> *There I return*

Your spirit fingers push us
to incant witness to your body
Feet pointed east
where sun stains sky
crimson and gold
Hands cradling your precious
brown belly
Hair pulled into a ponytail
like a river of obsidian

Our muscles arc rainbows
Spiral galaxies around you
Rock your lost flesh
Bare you up open-palmed
Sacred

III

Our homelands grow fertile
from our blood
sprout abundance
Feed multitudes
while we daily count our disappeared

What is breath
if it cannot hurl storms across the continent

What are words
that can't block blows
shade you from sun's white light
like large merciful wings

Drop cool sweet water
into your mouth
Stop blood's flow into dust

We count preciousness daily
Hold you as warriors
brothers
sisters
Hold you
with words and breath

Rise
in beauty

IV

The shocking whirl
of your hair and fingerprints
mimics wind that gives us breath

You are the rustle of leaves
whirlwinds of dust
feathered smoke rising from sage

We will sew you a gown of white shells
threaded with yellow zigzag lightning

Adorn you with black clouds
brush blue corn pollen across your lips
braid thunder through your hair

We will be your breath
We will be your song

V

It is finished in beauty
It is finished in beauty

In memoriam: F. C. Martinez Jr.

PART TWO

Love/Medicine

Maurice Kenny

My First Book

The only one
he ever gifted
me with
was a paperback
copy of
Tarzan:
Man of the Apes,
my first naked man.

I have it still,
re-read it a year ago,
remembered
how important
it was to my dreams
then and now,
dreams of all
the naked men
I've touched.

Chip Livingston

Ghost Dance

I think I'm going crazy when I see my reflection in the camera's lens. I'm surrounded by the dead. Jimi, Marilyn, Joan—face covered in cold cream, hand holding wire hanger high above her head. The Halloween Parade has paused for television crews in front of The Revolver on Duvall Street in New Orleans. I duck inside for a drink, take the elevator to the thirteenth floor.

I walk inside the club without ID. Tonight I don't need it. Tonight I'm invisible. I pass witches, goblins, boys dressed like ghouls. Once we were two of them. Once we both joined the annual masquerade. But tonight is different. Tonight I don a plain white sheet with ink. Circles traced around holes cut out to see through. Another hole through which I drink, from which I breathe.

I wasn't coming out tonight. Didn't plan or purchase a costume. Wouldn't wear one hanging in your closet. What led me to the linens then, to quickly cut a cotton sheet into a kid's uniform? What drove me to this?

Beneath this sheet, your medicine bag hangs around my neck, the tanned leather pouch you made me promise never to open. This is the first time I've worn it. But no one can see it. No one can see me.

I finish my drink, scotch neat, with a gulp, sing the invisible song you taught me, set the glass on the black wood rail, and, still singing, step onto the dance floor.

Beneath this sheet, I imitate you dancing. My feet, awkward at first, soon find your rhythm, and my legs bounce powwow style in the steps we both learned as kids. The steps that never left you. I dip and turn between, around the fancy dancers in their sequin shawls and feather boas. I shake my head like you did when your hair was long, the way you flipped it, black and shining, to the heavy beat of house music. The music hasn't changed much in case you're wondering. I dance in your footsteps; sing the invisible song; close my eyes.

When I open my eyes, I swear I see Carlo. Impossible, right, but he's stuffed inside that Nancy Reagan red dress and he's waving at me, sipping his cocktail and smiling. He's talking to Randy, who's sticking out his tongue that way he always did whenever he caught someone staring at him. I start to walk over but I bump into Joan.

She's glaring at me. Or it may just be the eyebrows, slanted back with pencil to make it look like she's glaring at me. She reaches past me and grabs Marilyn by her skinny wrist and pulls her away, but Carlo and Randy are gone. Where they stood are faces I don't recognize. Faces dancing. Masks, I realize. Faces behind masks.

The DJ bobs furiously with pursed lips, headphones disguised as fiendish, furry paws, in the booth above the floor. He introduces a new melody into the same harping beat, and I remember to dance. I remember you dancing. My fingers sliding across your sweaty chest, I find the necklace. The sheet clings to my body in places. The new song sounds just like the last song but I'm being crowded together with strangers. I can no longer lift my legs as high as I want to, so I sway in place, shuffle with the mortals on the floor.

Behind me someone grabs me, accidentally perhaps, but I turn violently, jealously. There are too many people in this equation. Two become one again and again, and ones become twos. All around me real numbers add up to future possibilities. Imaginary numbers. It's why we're here dancing.

A cowboy nods his hat in my direction. But he can't be nodding at us. We're invisible. I think maybe he is a real ghost; he's peering intently into the holes cut out for my eyes. He looks like Randolph Scott, blond and dusty, so I look around for Cary Grant as Jimi lifts the guitar from his lips and wails. Randolph Scott is coming this way and I turn my back and dance.

I want you back, Elan. I want you back dancing beside me. I start chanting this over and over to myself. *I want you back. I want you back.*

You taught me the power of words. I believed you. I can even smell you now. Sandalwood oil and sweat. I turn and expect to see you.

Not you behind me.

Not you beside me.

Not you in front of me.

Not you anywhere around me.

I make my way to the bar, but the bar is too crowded. The barman's face grimaces over hands holding folded dollars as he tries to keep the glasses filled. The air is thick with bitter smoke. It's hard to breathe. I make my way for the door, notice the cowboy trailing me. In the elevator, I go down alone.

Into the rain on Duvall Street, we walk out together. One set of footprints splashes our muddy way toward home, then, turning, I realize we are not going home, but passing more pagan tricksters decked out as holiday spirits.

The bells in the clock tower tell me it is midnight. Squeaking from its hinges, the door to morning slowly opens and it's All Saints Day, the Day of the Dead, and I am walking toward Boot Hill, to where you are buried.

We're alone in the cemetery. And the wind lifts the rain in a mist rising up from the wet earth which is claiming me. I remove my sheet in front of the cement memorial that holds your body up above the boggy ground. I remove my shoes. I strip off everything except your leather pouch around my neck, and I dance for you. My legs are free and I whirl and sing.

I'm dancing for you now, because you loved to dance. I want you back dancing. I want you dancing now.

I'm dancing for you now, because you loved to dance. I want you back dancing. I want you dancing now.

I'm dancing for you now, because you loved to dance. I want you back dancing. I want you dancing now.

I'm dancing for you now, because you loved to dance. I want you back dancing. I want you dancing now.

Michael Koby

Come Back to the 5 & Dime Jimmy Dean, Jimmy Dean

. . . he fell on his face and did reverence . . .

—2 SAMUEL 9:6

. . . he fell on his face and laughed . . .

—GENESIS 17:17

The old lady said, "There's talk of rebuilding in time."
"Time is such a nebulous date to wait for,"
said the girl who used to be a boy.
And the other girl, Sandy Dennis, who was always a girl
and had raised their child in a Texas drought,
said, "Shhh . . . listen . . . a slowly passing train is so romantic."

Were we ever a proud group?
Hadrian and Antinous?
What have the plague years done to us men?

Today, cleaning the house
The telephone rang
and thinking it may be my mother,
a telemarketer, a bill collector—
I didn't answer, but let
the machine get it.
And there was your voice,
with our message,
"We're not here right now, but . . ."
And not bothering to listen for the incoming caller—
having lived for weeks here alone
while you are away on business—
I, morbid as a Victorian, thought
shouldn't we record our *"I love you's,"*

just in case one of us was shut up,
gone forever?

Why, this spring, am I feeling so unsettled—
Dragging my feather duster 'cross the tabletops,
spitting the blues?
An hour till your soap opera,
the one I make fun of you for watching,
with not enough time
to find the right words?

I'd want words with double meaning—
bloom, light, wave—
words I could string together
to make something
precious, fancy.

But we are healthy!

HIV negative and not even a cold—
I will make tea,
be your surrogate while you are away—
watch your silly soaps for you.
Perhaps the television will quiet me
numb this doe-dumb brain
so it can handle the housecleaning,
the cats, the phone calls.

You know I would,
if I had the time or patience—
plait a chain of my hair,
if I had any hair left,
into some memento.
Glue seashells into a valentine.
Make you a nest of words.

William Raymond Taylor

Something Wants To Be Said

Duane, how are you? I owe you a letter, my favorite cynic, a cynic
Who played hopeful for me, your young lover, wary of scaring me off
With the bitterness that edged your heart. The white world was your
 enemy
Has that changed? You said a lot of people in Oklahoma look like me,
It was reassuring. I owe you a letter, I owe you an explanation
Why I turned away when the pleasure in my body mirrored yours and
 your words
Rang with integrity. How I loved your mind! Yet when we sat down
To that salmon dinner, my voice froze in my chest—a mystery. You
 did not know
Or understand why I turned cold, and I could not explain. Perhaps
It was your insistent suggestion of penetrating me, perhaps
It was the appetite of your smile. Something touched the permanent
 shadows
Of the sexual assault I endured as a child, making me
Unable to open my vulnerability to you. I hesitate even now to risk my
 heart,
Broken so many times. *Something wants to be said*, you spoke through
 the receiver
Of my telephone, two weeks later, but nothing would come.
I owe you a letter, but there's too much I cannot say.

Malea Powell

A *meditation partially composed in a D.C. coffeehouse because there isn't anything better to do in this city of dead white fathers. . .*

for jeff, the best jewish punk rock guitarist avant-garde poet I know

You said, "if it was up to me i'd have muffins *and* eggs" a mere three months after you left before they were even finished and now I can stop thinking about muffins, about how i too often feed you leftovers from meals eaten with other not-quite-not-lovers and your mouth i could make some analogy here about muffins and lovers but i don't have the patience for it as i sit here in this coffeehouse and smell death and destruction all around—*in this temple as in the hearts of the people for whom he saved the union the memory of abraham lincoln is enshrined forever*—monument to a president who hanged dakotas fuck sometimes perplexity has exactly the color and taste of kiwi eaten with the skin on, a fuzziness that hangs on your teeth until you spit it out and pretend it's a perfectly normal thing to do banana nut muffins—a symphony of colonialism like that phone conversation from mt. adams—miles' wild horn and your steady georgia o'keeffe grey-line voice telling me a hundred-year-old story about dead pigs, cincinnati slaughterhouses, & ohio rivers as i meditate on the geometry of your mouth against mine until it leaks into "i'd really like to see you" oh yeah, muffins kitchens coffee cats and gardens and lush life descendant-ing towards absolute perplexity kiwi again which is nothing like this half-finished pile of hummus, kalamatas, and bread, the remains of a meal eaten in a city built on blood and bones and stolen swamp-land except you know the other night when i was smoking a borrowed cigarette i said "everybody leaves—you take what you can get" and alex laughed russia into the orange air of thursdays at the treetop that was something like muffins, something like the pepperoncini strewn about this plate, something like the ghosts screaming round dupont circle, something like the truth except for how i don't believe it is there such a thing as a geometry of trust would it be non-euclidean or does it follow the rules of rockabilly, of strings pulled by fingers careful against my throat—as careful as when you made those tex-mex eggs but hey, that's weeks after this coffeehouse ok, muffins and kiwi and the fine equation of all i don't know suddenly in a heap of tangled wires at our feet as we cook and eat and stare and talk across a continent unconquered, undiscovered that exists only in the pause between drumbeats and makes me ache for an escape from holocausts even though that's almost all we have in common, that genocide assimilation story well that and muffins . . .

Qwo-Li Driskill

Love Poem, After Arizona

Baby
let me press my palm
against your chest
staunch the flow
of despair that beats from
your sacred heart
like an oil spill

We are two mixed-blood boys
and know empires are never gentle
Take off your Mexica mask
so I can see your beloved
Nahua face
Remove your wooden shield
so I can kiss your
Apache sternum
taste in your sweat
the iron of Spain
that never conquered us

There is too much time for war
Outside they
erect walls
hone laws

imagine gods
sharp and white
as history

But we have poetry
we have song
we have the stubble of your chin
I kiss as I reach
under the armor
of your white t-shirt
hold hard
your heart's
warm beat

The veins in your arms
turquoise roads
my tongue traces
to paths older than
metal fences

Your hands
like butterfly wings
disrupt
smooth air
gather momentum
until our gasps birth hurricanes
no law can stop

Baby
curl into the crook of my arm
rest your head here
on my chest

Just for tonight
forget wars
waged against us

Handsome
our lips will skim
this dark
outside the rule of law

We reweave the order of the universe
dream away borders
awake
to the light
of a continent

Maurice Kenny

He's watched

ONE

He's watched
            passing the window
each winter/summer.
January hides the flesh
but reveals
            struggle
climbing the snow
            covered hill
            sidewalk.
July he carries
            the T-shirt
in hands which swat flies
pecking sweaty skin.
His work pants
            (belted waist)
hang below his navel
                and expose black hairs
glistening,
            dew on the belly.
Not a word is passed
                between

January or July
            though
eyes speak and hands.

The passing is fast
                as
truth knows:
excitement
blazes,
propels the hurried
                walk
up the hill
            to the window eyes.

TWO

Black hairs rise from the crotch
warming the beauty of manhood;
seep a straight line up the flat
belly, circle purple nipples.

Face bronzed, brows sparrow wings
shade brown eyes rich in wonder
when mouth consumed essence.

THREE

Legs strong birch;
arms oak;
vision high as white pine;
beauty . . . an autumnal tamarack.

FOUR

A naked light would expose
                the lie . . .
Indeed youth is wasted on the young

old and wise ones say.
                    Not true!
Beautiful youth is only wasted
                              for the old.

FIVE

Fingers play in dark curls
coiled to clutch and hold;
Mouth, lips smell lime flavored,
peach tongue cannot cool.
continence:
                    chickory spring.

Moonless night
at the edge of the dark lake
was kind:
eyes could not see
or forget
hair was turning grey.

SIX

It is better than not.
It is better than nothing.
Often more safe than to.
Love is dangerous,
                    fatal
in more ways than just a broken heart
which is abstract
as a heart cannot break.
Touch the brown cheek,
scent a lime mouth
or plum nipple.
First anguish.
Disappointment. maybe.
Betrayal is possible.

Eventually pleasure
                    of savoring
old experiences, mouths,
thighs, belly tinged
by fine black hairs;
lust, lush, reciprocated.
Better than not.
Better than nothing.

Saves anguish, saves pain,
Saves the cold, emptiness.
Fires forever loins.
Burnt dreams.
Better than nothing, than not.
Allow feathers of memory
to tease and fulfill
Abstain, indulge, tickle
the imagination
                    vision.
Night light is no more kinder
than dawn, sunrise;
no more considerate
than truth.

SEVEN

Steps. Foot by foot steps
the climb of the hill
where windows stare
out at twilight, eve
empty, bare.
          Hide behind the drape.
Think. Better than not.

Jaynie Lara (Weye Hlapsi)

Being Two Spirit

What does it mean to be "Two Spirit"?
Walking in the land of our ancestors,
Walking with our hearts open,
Walking close to Creator,
Walking with passion,
yet hiding who we are.

Today I go to a powwow,
wishing in my heart
to be a Switch Dancer;
Eating fry bread and laughing
with my people.

Deep in my heart,
I want to walk hand in hand
with my love,
as we play and sing on the powwow trail.
I want my love sitting behind me,
as I sing the songs of my elders and honor our ancestors.

Two Spirit is who I am.
I pick and choose which of my
people to tell.
My love has held me at night,

kissed me as I cry over
comments made about who I am.

I sing the songs with my sisters,
hiding, laughing, crying,
while gazing at my sweetheart's soft lips
and the tenderness of her smile.
I dare to put my arms around the woman
who loves me for who I am.
I watch the stares and hear the whispers carried in the air.

Daniel David Moses

Lament Under the Moon

On the lookout beside
the wide river of night,

seeing how the moon's
reflection swims, I'd rather

be certain about where
in mid current, in mid

crossing you are. So far
ahead—though you're younger—

into and through the waning
light. Too soon you'll dive

underwater, try with
one breath to reach the far

shore and not leave the moon
crazy in your wake. You

can't wait for me. Too late,
too late. Too soon you'll rest

beyond the moon, another
great bear made of stars.

James Thomas Stevens

Thames

Always these multiple entrances
                to the underground
                            descending.

Fearing a missed reunion,
I earlier reconnoiter.

But you are there, on Baker Street,
        le printemps ascending.
Then fumbling embraces
        as you lead me back
                down.

Ever traversing *us*.
The many spans that separate.

Westminster. Hungerford. Waterloo. Blackfriars. Or leaving Saint Paul's
to cross the Millennium.

At nightfall reflected
in London's revolving eye.

Once more finding,
        once again above a river,
                Nous sommes dans notre bulle.

And staring off to Battersea,
watching night trains cross the river,
I think of Turner's *Rain, Steam and Speed.*

How diligently we'd searched
        the canvas for a rabbit,
                fleeing a steam-engine on Maidenhead Bridge.

And I am reminded that there is always a rabbit.
              Some frightened fancy fleeing zigzag before us.

St. Catherine's Docks and the Catherine wheel.
Here, forever turning
        above the grey embankment.

Always walking on water, we
move to the foot
        of Westminster Bridge.

You tell me to
      Look up.
From this,
your favoured place, where time
is framed
        between the statuary and sycamore.

And resting on a bench
we become
        alchemical.

Four iron leonine feet and four
of flesh and bone.

All mythological union, twin headed, two backed, and many armed.

The spiny seed balls of a sycamore
dance mournfully before us.

Flight-denied
        and tethered to the trees.

Cheryl Savageau

Deep Winter

I wanted to kiss your neck
in the middle of traffic
but instead I just brushed your cheek
we'd been eating Greek food
avgolemono, moussaka, hot
flatbreads with olive oil and feta
I wanted to kiss you then
in falling snow, bring on
an early thaw

PART THREE

Long/Walks

Janice Gould

We Could Not Forget

The journey began, and the soldiers trudged all around us
that fall they stole us from our homeland.
We had a great distance to cover.
We left everything, all that we held familiar.

That fall they stole us from our homeland,
having herded us into corrals for cattle.
We left everything, all that we held familiar—
the granite rocks of the canyon, the buckeye and laurel.

Having herded us into corrals for cattle,
the soldiers were nervous we'd escape and posted armed guards.
The granite rocks of the canyon, the buckeye and laurel
whispered prophetic stories we could not forget.

The soldiers were nervous we'd escape and posted armed guards.
They trained their guns on us. Just at sunrise the winds arose and
whispered fearful stories we could not forget.
In a storm of dust and tears we began our trek.

They trained their guns on us. Just at sunrise the winds arose and
warned us not to flee, not to resist.
In a storm of dust and tears we began our trek,
men, women, and children, angry and afraid. The soldiers

charged us not to flee, not to resist.
So we stumbled tired, hungry, through valley heat,
men, women, and children. Angry and afraid, the soldiers
pushed us along, impatient with our tears.

So we stumbled tired, hungry, through valley heat.
We had a great distance to cover.
Pushed along, impatient with our tears,
our journey began, and the soldiers trudged all around us.

Laura M. Furlan

Our Wars

I was born during the Vietnam War. If there are memories in my blood, what should I remember? My father, who is still only a voice on the phone, was in the war. Special Forces, secret missions. He was a P.O.W. but he doesn't talk about it. He does tell me about family fortunes hidden in caves. Our family's fortune. My fortune, he says. He whispers the directions. Just in case. Write this down.

It's the post-traumatic stress, I know. But where does his truth end and the paranoia begin? I often think about following the directions to that cave, if it's there. What would I find? Of what does my fortune consist? Are there documents and artifacts that link our family to some historical past? Photographs or deeds or jewels? What would he choose to hide there?

He's recently disappeared again. Off the radar. His phone disconnected. I know that he's returned to Mississippi, where our family has lived for four generations or more. I wonder what it was like to come home from the war in foreign lands. Mississippi is that foreign to me, the land that holds the bones of my ancestors, in Chickasaw County, in Pascagoula and Tupelo and Red Land. The homeland. Would I remember this place? Could I sit on the veranda, talk about old times? Would I be able to whistle Dixie?

Dan Taulapapa McMullin

The Act of Memory in Laguna California

Lifting memory and wet planks, the scent of reef, moss, and story
My grandfather Nimarota in Samoa with paddle, sail, and brother
    fisherman
Out of sight of home, to bring shark liver and pink seaweed
To his eldest child, my mother, a little girl then
Waiting barefoot on the beach, eighty years ago
Here in Amelika a young man's homecoming from Iraq
Cutting yellow ribbons from the palm trees, among tall red white and
    blue candles
Sharing home video of Baghdad, red figures against black
As seen through a tank turret night sight, now on the big screen teevee
Dodging dead dogs stuffed with bombs, or sacks of rice
A youth who says with a relish that he has killed, now
In the same old chair, an erection always half hidden in his pants
Now turning the pages of his photo album, teal flowers prepared by
    his girlfriend
Who sent him a camouflage teddy bear she made at the teddy bear
    store
When he squeezed its paw he heard her voice at night
Among dusty bunks, in Saddam's old tank turret factory
A mural of the old man and a child, faces shot through for target
    practice
I take the album from my youngest niece and she cries
Not to see her brother sitting on the chest of a dead sniper

Who did not have the advantage of laser sighting
Just a red dot on his nose bridge by the left eye
And pages of young shirtless American men lifting weights
There the recorded muezzin's song and a telephone voice from
    Kansas
For they who do not walk the sidewalks alone or sit in restaurants
The last photograph with a family of Iraqi men saying goodbye
His uniform among their civilian clothes, their faces looking so like his
As if homecoming day was there

Indira Allegra

Blue Covers

Anyone who's been molested got wings
we who lean forward while walking
raise and wrap our shoulders like blankets
around hearts that beat out concave chests

we who lean forward while walking
blue covers and mirrors for feathers
around hearts that beat out concave chests
scattered floor to door

blue covers and mirrors for feathers
souls lost turn lamps heavy
scattered floor to door
missing pages of journals growing

souls lost turn lamps heavy
raise and wrap our shoulders like blankets
missing pages of journals growing
Anyone who's been molested got wings

Qwo-Li Driskill

(Auto)biography of Mad

Subject Index

Abuse, Physical, ii, 3;
    Sexual, Age 4; 28,
    Age 14; 53,
    Age ?; ix, 4, 10, 14, 28, 25, 53,
    55, 98, 116–123;
    Psychic, i-xx, 94–106;
    Verbal, i–17. *See also*
    Rape

Bipolar Disorder, 16, 23, 28, 400,
    1593;
    Bipolar Disorder, coping
    mechanisms;
    aromatherapy; 630,
    running in circles, 403;
    screaming into pillows, 45;
    self-medication, 520–2100;
    listening to radios in
    dark rooms; 504–506

Cemeteries. *See* Golf
    Courses, Trail of Tears,
    Middle Passage

Colonization, ix, 4, 10, 14, 25,
    28, 53, 55, 98, 116–123, 326,
    1492, 1540, 1838
Canton, South Dakota, xii, 263,
    432
Craziness. *See* Drapetomia,
    Hiawatha Asylum for
    Insane Indians,
    Madness, Post-Traumatic
    Stress Disorder (PTSD)

Depression, 12–28.
    See also Bipolar
    Disorder, Disability,
    Madness
Disability, 4, 10, 14, 16, 23, 25,
    26–29, 128, 200.
    See also Bipolar
    Disorder, Eugenics,
    Forced Sterilization,
    Madness, Post-Traumatic
    Stress Disorder (PTSD)
Drapetomia, x, xii, 264, 432, 1851

Nightmares, x, xii, 4, 10, 14, 128, 263–264, 432, 1492, 1540, 1838, 1989

Panic Attacks. *See* Madness, Post-Traumatic Stress Disorder (PTSD)
Psychological Disorders. *See* Bipolar Disorder, Drapetomia, Post-Traumatic Stress Disorder (PTSD)
Post-Traumatic Stress Disorder (PTSD), 4, 10, 14, 25, 26–29, 128, 200, 1492, 1533, 1838–1839

Rape, ix, 4, 10, 14, 25, 28, 53, 55, 98, 116–123, 1492, 1540, 1838; anal, ix, 4, 14, 26–28; oral, ix, 4. *See also* Abuse, Sexual; Colonization; Middle Passage, Slavery, Trail of Tears, Trauma,

Sexual; Post-Traumatic Stress Disorder (PTSD)

"Shell Shock." *See* Post-Traumatic Stress Disorder (PTSD)
Slavery, iv, 1492–1865. *See also* Abuse, Colonization, Drapetomia, Eugenics, Middle Passage, Trauma

Trail of Tears. *See* Cemeteries
Trans-Atlantic Slave Trade. *See* Middle Passage
Trauma Historical, 1492, 1540–1839; Physical, 1492; Psychic, 1492; Sexual, 4, 14, 28–29, 53, 1492, 1540–1839. *See also* Abuse, Sexual; Post-Traumatic Stress Disorder (PTSD)

Michael Koby

The Witch's House

John Fisher gave me the dead bat in a mason jar for Valentine's. I had accepted it, trying to be cool, fully aware that my hands were trembling against the jar glass. I knew that boys were into these things so I tried to be cool. I puffed up my chest and crossed my arms, remembering that this is how my dad stood. Legs buckling, I was trying to keep the position right. I remember thinking, "This is what boys do for you when they love you." I ran as far as I could, trying not to break the glass, knowing somehow that this dead nest of hair was meant for me, that I had always owned it. I wrapped it up in an old pillowcase, put it under my bed next to a couple of my dad's *Playboys*.

Spotted by those old trees, the black two-story stood across the field from our house. You could see it when you got on the bus. We all said it was black, but it was more dark brown, paint peeling and flaking in that abandoned farmhouse way, exposing the gray wood beneath. All us kids knew not to walk 'cross the field and step on that lawn, we had all tried. We knew that no matter how you tiptoed she would see you, there all the time, her head stuck in the window. She lived in that window. Once John camouflaged himself clumsily in his father's hunting jacket, the kind that make you invisible in the woods. Across the field he hid behind the trunk of an elm, painted white round the base. He peeked round the tree. We made bets if he would pee himself. I thought for sure he would pee. Right away that screen door opened, framing the lady with the long hair, hair my momma had said was ". . . a bit strange, hanging down to her backend like a Baptist in the wilderness." It bugged us, drove us nuts. Hers was the only spot of deep woods we weren't allowed to play in. No one ever got past that field without getting caught, not even Fisher.

She held on to that oversize jacket of his daddy's and kept it tight as she spoke, white spittle forming at the corners of her mouth, "Children that disobey go to hell and sizzle like pork rinds in oil. Thou shalt not . . . Thou shall not . . . Thou shall not," she sputtered.

I thought about Mamma clipping dozens of coupons to get that golden commandments charm bracelet, how all ten had turned her wrist green. I didn't know her sweet Jesus and I hated the idea of sizzling and popping like a piece of pigskin. Eventually she let Fisher loose and we all ran past the field and kept on till our tiny rib bones ached. Fisher's eyes watering, he looked older to me somehow as he stripped down to his white briefs, his underwear all yellow as he slid them off and threw them to the grass. As he pulled his feet back into his ruined pants, I wondered about Jesus. I was pretty sure he was just like the Easter Bunny or the Boogie Man or just a tool to frighten children who still believed in that stuff. I had feared that rabbit, red-eyed and laughing, laying plastic eggs on the grass.

Fortunately my dad had told me early on, reclining in his chair and drinking a beer, that everything my mom said about Tooth Fairies and Reindeers was utter bull. Still, I was kinda scared of dying, not all that certain whether I would fizzle in a fryer or not.

Once school started we abandoned our longing to drive the old lady nuts. We settled on telling ghost stories, sneaking into unfinished houses for a subdivision that went belly up, and smashing pennies on the railroad track. On the third day of school, I waited for the bumblebee of a bus. Through my horribly thick glasses, I saw two girls climbing down the steps of the crazy lady's house. We had never heard or seen children anywhere near that house. But out they stumbled in matching buttercup dresses, one as short as a Technicolor munchkin, the other awkwardly tall. Up the black rubbery steps, swiftly plopping down, I pressed my face against the window. The glass was spotted with bugs, yet I could see their descent. I knew something had to be wrong with them. Maybe they were kept captive in the root cellar or were new arrivals to the house, freshly kidnapped from some nice lady down at the Moo and Oink's meat counter who had carelessly turned her back to find a piece of meat with the least amount of whitish fat on it.

They entered, the tallest one smirking, mumbling to herself as she made her way to the back of the bus. All the cool kids were scared; I could tell because they didn't say a peep. I looked around as she unblinkingly intruded on their inner sanctum of high-top sneakers, stone-washed jeans, and Aquanet hairspray bangs. These were the kids my friends and I tried never to make eye contact with; we were all too poor to do that, live in the shopping mall, all big hair and hot pretzels. Following the tall girl was the shortest girl I had ever seen, who had somehow come to live in that horrible house. She stood right in the aisle, staring at me. Her mouth was moving, emitting a series of high-pitched bleeps. After I realized she was speaking English and asking if she could sit, I nodded.

She had an old lunchbox, the kind my dad took to work, a red and green plaid design rusted all around. She kept it on her lap. Her feet didn't touch the floor, they just dangled as she sat there quiet, her head barely touching the middle of the green leathery seat. Trying not to stare directly, I kept glancing left to right. She looked too normal to have come from that place. Tight red curls and hundreds of freckles.

"I'm Shelley," she said.

I dumbly smiled, knowing I would stumble over my own name. Knowing freckles meant Shelley was good no matter where she came from, Mamma said so, that freckles were a sign of wholesomeness, I relaxed a little. I didn't have freckles. I never had any. She didn't seem to mind.

After, we became friends, creating worlds while the other kids played hopscotch during recess. . . . We understood one another; we led similar lives built upon that hopeful hopelessness of daydreams. Around Halloween, Shelley got sick. Mrs. Eldridge, our teacher, who left red lipstick kisses on your cheeks after paddling you, asked me to take the ill Shelley her homework after school. I didn't like the idea, going to that house, but I agreed, making my pinched and pulled cheeks form a smile.

Counting the power lines from my space by the window, knowing I was close to home, I imagined what it would be like to have to cross that yard choked with weeds. It took the bus driver, Mrs. Knight, her shiny perm and white teeth, three times to get my attention. I stepped out, hurrying a little, knowing if you stayed in one spot of the field for a second too long, your shoes would sink and flood with water.

I felt like I was dying; I heard my mother's voice in my head, she reassured me that I wouldn't. When I got to the ripped screen door and knuckles white knocked, faint sounds of shoes scraping floorboards and then nothing. Then there she was, the Witch, Shelley's mother, staring straight down at me. I tried to speak, but I couldn't, I just looked up at her, unable to move. Behind her I saw Shelley, she was sprawled out on the couch, a washcloth on her forehead, red hair flat with sweat, raising a weak hello.

The Witch spoke, "I saw you coming up that lawn. Shelley told me you invited her to your heathen party. Well, she can't go Haloweenin'. She's sick, but even if she wasn't, she couldn't go. You believe me, only devil worshipers believe in trick or treatin'. . . . Those her books? Leave um right there on the stoop." And I did. I hopped off the porch and ran. A few yards away I looked back. She was still looking at me with those big black eyes. Quickening my steps, crossing the field without a chance of getting my shoes wet, found my way safe to our door. I turned around. She was still staring from behind that screen, her face like a headstone.

The next day, Shelley's sister, Margot, got on the bus, same buttercup dress, and her head almost hitting the ceiling. She sat down by me, her knees pushing against mine. Fisher, two seats behind me, was calling my name; I pretended not to notice. He shot a rubber band at my head, it hurt, but I let it bounce to the floor.

"Don't feel too bad about walking 'cross the lawn," she said.

"I don't like prayin'. Last night, Mamma caught me watching T.V. at our cousin's house again. There was this movie about a young girl forced to work in a gentlemen's club. They took dirty pictures of this girl, made her drink orange soda with pills in it."

Margot taught me how to dance like a stripper that day on the playground swing set. Using the poles supporting the metal roped swings, we each took turns showing the curious boys our routine. She was better at it than me, but I was a boy so I figured that was okay. We practiced for what seemed like forever, making full arcs under the sun and squint of their eyes. I started speaking to Fisher again, deciding it was okay if he loved me, as long as he never told anybody.

Eventually, the town condemned that house across the field as a danger, something about mold. I watched the family pack from our kitchen window, all of them in the same old dresses, hurrying around and stirring up dust. I was told they moved across town and that the girls were at a different school. The day they tore the house down, the dishes shook in the kitchen. I ran out to see what the racket was. Bulldozers dozing the house, the Witch's patchwork curtains fell as the roof caved in. My feet sinking in the mud, the leveled house standing there, wood planks jutting out like a shipwreck, abandoned socks scattering the lawn.

My ma phoned everybody on the block to spread the good news. For years the field stood bare, a black square where the house had stood. The neighbor kids took over this spot each Halloween, erecting a scarecrow dressed like the Wicked Witch. At night, if the wind was right, looking out your window, you could see it moving, slow and deliberate. Once on a dare, feet aching from trick or treating, I crossed that field. I stumbled and dropped my plastic fangs in the mud. Brushing them off as best as I could, drooling a little, I put them back in my mouth. I went up to that scarecrow and stole her pointy polyester hat and crossed the field back to my house. I hid the hat under my bed, next to the ashy bat, not quite knowing what they meant.

Daniel David Moses

Ballad of the Raft

—*Come on*, the big kid laughed, *Come on and try*
to do it. He stood unsteadily up
on the raft. Standing below, already

in to your chin, your underwater heart
tugged out toward him. Your head you held back, up
in the air about the depths that must have

been there below the raft, below the big
kid's ruckus. Just how did those depths compare
to the ones in blue black hair? Did you dare

what the little boy in you and that kid
of the raft wanted? How far up over
head would the river rise if you didn't

quite make it?—*Want them to know you're yellow?*
The kid was rocking the raft, punching out
waves, but what hit the young man in your head

in the chest was this tease. So out into
the stream you pushed, pulling the boy inside
along the undulating wake your heart

made of the blue black current. When he bobbed
up, a laugh at the side of the raft, no
part of you was ready for what came next.

He was grabbed by the hair—by that big kid,
yes—grabbed and held under. Where did your heart,
up in the air at last, go then? Into

the wave of laughter that crossed your face too?
—once you thrashed back to the surface, somehow
in the shallows. The outside guy, did he

nod, agree, that water in the eyes, up
noses, was funny? Meanwhile the part
inside, the little boy, refuses still

to mourn. He's found your underwater heart
at the bottom of the stream and dreams of
reviving the drowned. His fists pound the mud.

Maurice Kenny

Contacts

They say that D.C. is always sweltering hot as pancakes on a grill . . .
though that is something of a tired description. But it's hot, sticky, and
today pretty dusty. Never been here before . . . but that's the word, report
on the weather. There he was strolling half naked down the center of
Massachusetts Avenue as though he was the chief of the entire old con-
tinent. The protest march was heading toward the Washington Monu-
ment. Many Feathers—that's what he called himself in public, but his
American name was simply John Ursoil—wore a headband which gath-
ered the sweat from the march and held six feathers, one each for the
Iroquois Nations, and claimed Seneca. He was covered in sweat. It dripped
off his chin.

We happened to ride the charter bus together to D.C. Well, not really
together. I knew him pretty well but not so well I'd buy a bus ticket and sit
next to him for a six-hour ride. We just shared the bus as he sat three rows
in front as I had taken a seat towards the back. That was crazy. I'd worked
the night and was darn sleepy and thought I'd catch some Z's back there.
Wrong. It's the noisiest section of the bus. And who'd you suppose was
making most of the noise? Yep, you're right—none other than John Ursoil.

"Why we got to demand that land. And you know I'm a trained lawyer,
lawyers in this land know the ropes and can get what is coming to them—
by hook or by look."

He did not even get the bromide correct.

"We are marching to honor the museum which they think they gave us.
They didn't give us a damn thing. Stole. Stole . . . Stole it. Right."

And his six feathers in the band wobbled as his head passionately wobbled proving points.

"I come on this Greyhound to these dirty capital streets in protest, not honoring, no celebration for their gift. Gift my Aunt Tillie. Where would they be without this Mother Earth, our Mother Earth. Squawking in London Ghetto, strapped to a guillotine in Paris, milking cows in Germany—poor, starving tenant farmers. Yeah. This is the land of milk and honey and I . . . "

My headset was in my tote bag and instantly was clamped to my ears. Dylan was a better sound, or even Morrison's beat.

He sat there three rows of seats ahead of me snorkeling like a whale. Actually, he looked like a whale, no, not really, more like a shark. But plump ripe in the belly for the plucking or harpooning. Naked from the waist up except for the war paint coloring his skin. No not tattoos but finger paint that would wash off the next morning. Across his shoulder was a golden snake; running from the neck to his navel, in a hairless belly button was a silver snake. Each side and below the shoulder were red stars and drops of white hail—somewhat reminiscent of the great Lakota Crazy Horse. His face was splotched with green painted feathers and like a circus clown his nose was painted purple. I think he was trying to hide the fact that he drank too much.

My headset shifted as the bus swerved around a sharp hairpin and again I heard the conversation of two Onondagas sitting directly in front of me.

"Listen to that fat oracle up there. If he is a lawyer then I'm the Peacemaker, and I've come to this land to bring 'The Great Message.' He's no lawyer . . . but a loud windbag."

This was definitely no way to speak of an elder and most surely not of your own nation. But, man, there is an end to what you can take I'd suppose.

I ruffled with my headset and just as I replaced it on my ears and the Dead struck up a chord, I heard him plunder the air with . . .

"Holy catfish . . . I don't eat catfish . . . they skim the river for the shit on the rocks. Clean the crap. But as I was saying."

I tuned out and refused to listen to his lecture on catfish which was a creature that did its job well and thanklessly. I fell sound asleep.

Later that night we arrived in Washington and were reacquainted with what we were to do in the celebration of the new museum the Feds, and I suppose the BIA, built with our sweat and monies. I went for a Whopper and coffee. Lo and behold there were a couple of folks from my tribe in a booth.

"Hey Frankie—sit down."

"Hey Injun Joe, Regretta. How you two doin'?"

We coffeed up. Sank a fry or two and gobbled a Whopper—and as always the talk went to Many Feathers.

"He just won't shut up."

Another Indian slid into the store, spotted us and came over, offered the Bear Shake, and took a seat in the booth.

"Talking about Many Feathers, huh."

"Everyone talks about him and nobody talks to him."

"'Cause he don't let you speak."

"Yeah. That's good Indian courtesy. Eh!"

"Yup."

"Says he's got a great war record from Alcatraz and Wounded Knee. Claims he took a bullet in the arm at the Old Church."

I could not contain my rage.

"Took a bullet at the church. He doesn't know what a church looks like, let alone the inside of a Longhouse," I said.

"Well, he's got pictures and newspaper articles cut out."

"So did Hitler," I added.

Regretta just giggled and listened to we guys drown him.

"He worked on *Akwesasne Notes* back in the seventies, he said."

"Yeah, well, I was there off and on, and I never saw him at the Nation House. That was for anyone who would come to the Reservation and shovel out the shithouse for a bowl of Jenny Shoe's corn soup."

I simply stared at this speaker, an Indian who had just taken a seat, a man somewhere in his early fifties, old enough to have been at *Notes*.

"In and out, I was. Nearly every week. We had bundles of people coming and going . . . probably lots of Feds . . . FBI. I never saw him there nor did he ride the White Roots of Peace bus 'cross country."

This Indian sounded fierce, no stoic he, and no kidder either. Short man, fairly dark, wrinkles around his eyes, not much of a chin as though he'd swallowed part of it. He wore a fleece jacket, orange, and had a turquoise ring on his right middle finger. He spoke sincerely and laid as honest a word on the air as any Red-Jacket might have.

"Don't trust his skin color. Says he's a full blood. But wait for him to take his contacts out. His eyes are as blue as that napkin holder there on the table."

"Blue, huh! Contacts do that?"

"Yes, sir," my friend the Onondaga man exclaimed, "and more than that."

I was getting plenty interested in this conversation. The tiredness felt on the bus had evaporated. I was all ears, no headset on now.

"Look at that crazy sons a bitch. Two snakes on his flesh. Hail fading, even his nose purples. Next, he'll be telling us he's a holy person or Chief Atotarho. He dressed up in tons of turquoise jewelry, squash blossom pendants, rings in his hairy ears. Look close to his flesh, just near the nipples."

"Why?" Regretta interjected.

"Force cut marks. He shaves his chest."

"Yeah, Indians don't have no body hair," I supplied the old joke.

"You're right." The flesh had been marred by a razor.

"Who is this guy? What is he up to?" I asked, beginning to weary.

I drank down my coffee and went to the counter for the refills and a piece of cherry pie.

"I'll tell you what," said Henry Miner, the Onondaga guy who sat down with us. "I'll tell you what. Rub under that paint and you will see white skin below the man's tan, blue eyes behinds the contacts. He's about as old as I am. I'm fifty-four. And I know him from somewhere else."

We all drank up our coffee and split for the night. I was to sleep on the charter bus.

The dawn fell a beautiful marigold. I'd never seen so many native people gathered. From an airplane we sure looked a mammoth garden of brilliant flowers. We marched, we sang, we danced, we spoke in a great, moving oratory and allowed an America to honor the Indian, our ancestors, and our glorious past. I thought, if we could still be tribal and truly sovereign. But . . . and *but* is a mammoth word, isn't it.

The day was glorious. Mother Nature and the Creator were obviously there and seeing everything was perfect as a human could make it.

Many people went into the new museum. How do I describe this phenomenon? Glorious is getting to be a stale word, and by the way it is a Christian word and probably shouldn't be used in connection with this celebration.

It was the Indian theme. A fantastic building out and inside. The honorable past and the present both were embodied. We felt we had at last won a war, and perhaps it would be the last war.

I was feeling great, proud of my red heritage and with my people . . . first. Then I looked to the steps, and holy crap there stood Many Feathers with his arm about the shoulder of a famous senator, one seen on TV too often, one who happened to be an Indian and a Republican.

"What the hell," I heard escape from my own mouth. At that moment Henry Miner sidled up to me.

"There's your man."

Henry was right, though Many Feathers was not my "man." Yet, there he stood with an arm about the senator's shoulder whispering words into the old man's ear. About what? Who could know. Some devious suggestion I would suppose. Something out of the pot for him, Many Feathers. Henry continued nudging me and speaking into my right ear.

The noise was great and many of his words were a syllable away by the waves of sounds—some happy and pleasing, others negative resulting from an inordinate amount of passing time in which the wait and weight for this honor to the American Indian. I know my teacher would say all good things come to those who wait, a bromide. America is a bromide which is synonymous with a lie.

"Yes, just about when I was a shaver. I think I saw this guy in a Syracuse bar, an Indian bar, Onondaga. It was a hot summer night. The bar was a block or so from the old Greyhound bus station. Dingy, scary part of town, naturally. It wasn't really safe to walk there—woman or man, drunk or sober."

He lit a cigarette. Pulled heavily the smoke and continued telling his tale.

"I was twenty-two and with my grandfather—now passed. The bar was crowded, but Grandpa had eagle sight and hawk ears. He picked up his frothy beer, sipped, placed it back on a wet bar, and staring through the heavy fog of cigarette smoke, his gaze cut through the thick clouds to observe a young guy open the door and enter our bar. He looked older than me. Was in a clean shirt, Levis, and worn shiny dress shoes. No hat, no coat or sweater, but looked heeled for someone on the street. He pushed his way through the dense crowd of Indians and managed the bar. Timid but fearless. Lost but looking for a home."

Henry's story was pulling me in and refusing to release my imagination.

"Why are you telling me this? Should I care?"

"Yes, you should care." He blew a trail of smoke.

"The guy—I thought he was white, Anglo, and he took a stand next to Grandpa and me. With his foot on the brass rail he called out for a bottle of Miller's. As the barkeep was real busy and could not just drop everything and run for this stranger, the new guy got a little huffy. 'No damn service in here?'

"Grandpa eyed him to the wood-shaves, which covered the floor with spit, stale beer, and something that looked like blood.

"'What's the rush, son. It's early.'

"'I got a thirst.' He attempted a smile.

"Grandpa looked him dead in the eye and asked: 'You Indian, boy?'

"He bounced his head in the air. He smiled, sort of snorted, lit a cigarette, and blew several puffs of smoke before answering.

"'Well!' Grandpa gestured with a 'heap' big smile as his own beers were getting to him.

"'I, I well, gosh, I guess I might be. My mama said we're a, we're a, yes, a Mohawk—she said.'

"'Mohawk,' Grandpa mimicked.

"'Yes, a Mohawk, Mohawk yes.'

"'Well, where from?'

"'Uh,' he stuttered, 'I guess from up here—north.'

"By then the bartender gave him a beer and the guy paid for a round for me and my grandpa, who was getting very interested in this guy.

"'Oh yeah, wadda know. Look like you have a sweat just shortly.'

"'Yes, Ia, Ia, yes.'

"'Up north?'

"He emptied his bottle while Grandpa smiled a foolish grin which it was his tease.

"'Yes, north.'

"'Which tribe.'

"'I just said—Mohawk.'

"'I know, but there are several tribes in the Mohawk Nation.'

"'Tribes?'

"'Yes, tribes. Several.'

"'It is all the same.'

"The blue eyes began to squint as if to hide; the cheek began to flush and his forehead to wrinkle.

"'Yes, tribe,' Grandpa reiterated.

"'Would you like another beer?' He called the barkeep, 'Set 'em up for these men.'

"But he did not answer the question.

"'I'm Indian, too. Mohawk.'

"'Son, I won't call you a liar, but you look white to me. But I'm drunk.'

"Several beers later we were all three pretty drunk and Grandpa was speaking Iroquoi to both of us.

"The barkeep called last beer.

"Grandpa said no more and winked at me. 'We better head for home.' And to the Mohawk guy: 'You got a place to sleep, son?'

"'I was going to stay in the bus station,' he replied.

"But it closed at 2 a.m. Grandpa invited him to our place. All three of us were so drunk we could hardly stand and would more than likely get lost looking for home.

"'Now that you're gonna sleep at my place you might tell me your name and offer a Bear Shake.'

"The kid didn't know what he meant by a Bear Shake let alone a sweat, or where Mohawks lived. But he came to the apartment with us, a matter of six blocks away.

"'George.'

"'No, I mean your Mohawk name.'

"He stopped dead in his tracks as though instantly petrified: 'George,' he said again, staggering as we weaved down the sidewalk.

"'George, huh. OK. That's good though it doesn't sound Mohawk to me.'

"We got home. Grandpa put 'George' on a pallet on the floor. Threw an old coat over him and turned out the light."

Here Henry made a long pause. He seemed forgetful or simply hesitant to continue.

"Surely it didn't end with the light out," I questioned.

"No, no it didn't end with the light out. As a matter of fact it is still going on." He lit another cigarette.

"Grandpa rises early. Says a traditional morning prayer to the Creator. In the old days he would have bathed in the river, but not then in the Syracuse water, old Salt City." He puffed.

I was going crazy for the end as it was due any moment.

"Grandpa finished his prayers. Went to wake up the guy, pulled off the coat, and pushed his butt with his right shoe.

"'Get up. Rise, son, and fly away. You're a bird with many feathers.'"

God! I nearly fell down. Grandpa!

Henry squashed out his cigarette and placed the butt in his coat pocket with others as if to say the Spam and peanut butter may not always be there to take home, so I keep the butts.

"And there he stands. Many Feathers, named by my full-blood Onondaga grandfather—the elder who taught me all. Many Feathers giving the white man's shake to that government official, a senator. Why not the Bear Shake? Why a shake at all?"

We shook hands—the Bear Claw. It was time for my charter Greyhound bus to take us home.

"George Many Feathers. I'll be a spotted pig."

Luna Maia

authentically ethnic

So this girl from Queens sends me a letter
lecturing me about the Native Americans and fry bread,
how it wasn't until federal rations that Indians made fry bread.
maybe I should have told her, that my tribe was not
federally recognized until the year I was born, so there were no
rations. maybe I should have told her, that my great-grandmother
didn't make fry bread, she made tortillas and pigeon soup,
a single mother with eight children all picking cotton
and washing clothes for survival, and No I don't think that is an
AUTHENTICALLY-ETHNIC TRADITION EITHER.
it was survival.
the history of my ancestors is about survival,
not being authentically ethnic.

My mother has fond memories of pigeon soup, and fresh
tortillas. I have my grandfather, taking me for walks to
Mexico City to buy pan dulce, the bakery was really only
five blocks away off Milpas Street in Santa Barbara,
but we always had that journey.

How can I call my myself a REAL Indian, when I have
tortillas and pan dulce in my vocabulary?
how can I call myself a REAL Mexican, when I have
French and German blood running through these
veins?

I am not real, to choose an identity is putting on a
costume, playing make believe.
I don't want to make you believe anything,
you already have it figured out for yourself.

Carrie House

Sweet Grass

One morning, I, Navajo, wake up in Tiwa country
Friend from Taos Pueblo tells me they just killed a buffalo
We drive up the hillside and see a tractor hoisting the buffalo
Ten people are standing around, looking at each other
I watch the tractor's rear wheels come up and off the ground
The operator soon notices and lowers the buffalo
A man cuts the buffalo open
Everyone looks around at each other
Someone asks, "Who here can butcher?"
Someone says, "She can, she's Navajo!"
I say, "Is this why he drove me up here?"
I ask for a wheelbarrow and a galvanized pail is placed down
I say, "This is for Minnie Mouse, where is a wheelbarrow or two!"
A wheelbarrow and several big buckets arrive
Two men open the cavity and I put my head and arms in
Steam from the inside smells of sweet grass
       I close my eyes and am overwhelmed by the sensation of being
       in a mother's womb
I carefully pull everything out and onto the wheelbarrow and
   buckets
Everything is huge; the heart, the kidneys, the book, the liver. . . .
My pocket knife is the sharpest knife in the group
One evening, I, Navajo, eat buffalo in Tiwa country

126

D. M. O'Brien

The Perfect Picture

We are driving along a prairie highway, in search of the Qu'Appelle Valley. For whatever reason, it is important to see this water in the middle of Saskatchewan. My mom, Evelyn, wants to see it because it has to do with a poem. Someone searching for some lost love, or something. Who knows? All I know is we are in her old Chevy listening to country music and the sky tries to touch the earth. And I know I have to tell her. Here, in the car, when I have her all to myself. She has to drive and I know she won't leave me in the middle of nowhere.

I drum my fingers on my new camera and look out the window for the perfect picture on the way. The clouds go on forever. The sunflower fields are stunning, but they are too happy for me. I need something darker. A trace of something lost.

"Whatchya brooding on over there, missy? We're supposed to be having fun."

Her idea of fun is her telling me that life isn't fair and I should just learn to accept that people suck. Oh, yeah, great fun. "Nothin'," I mutter.

"You know, your Uncle Mike used to say that to me all the time, too, but I always knew he was lying. You can't hide anything from me. I birthed you and watched you grow. Don't you know I know you better than you do?"

So she thinks. Do you know that I sleep with girls and that if a guy tried to kiss me I would throw up on him or punch him in the face? Not that any guy would want to kiss me. It's pretty obvious to them I'm a dyke. I should tell her that right now. She would be so shocked. She would see how wrong she is about me.

But I am too late, she has started talking again. "You know, when I was a teenager, I used to ride my bike for miles and miles. I would pack a lunch and ride all the way to Moose Jaw. Can you imagine that? You kids are too lazy these days to do that."

"Uh-huh."

"Tell me something, what are you going to do after you graduate?"

"What?"

"You know, graduate. What are you going to do after?"

"Oh, god, I don't know, Mom. Go to school somewhere."

I'm going to go to Montreal or Toronto and get involved in gayness and sleep with every girl in town. I'm going to . . . leave this place and never return. I'm afraid to leave. I'm afraid.

"Aha. Well, as long as you do something with yourself. Find a man eventually, have a couple babies. Have a life."

Here we go again. I have to tell her. I have to tell her now before she names my unborn children.

"Mom."

She drives for a couple of minutes before she finally says, "Yeah, what is it?"

"I think I'm gay."

I can't believe the words have come out, never to return to the safety of silence again. I can feel the car slow down a few kilometers. "You think? Aren't you supposed to know that sort of thing?"

"Well, I am. I know I am. I never liked boys. I don't think I ever will."

"But, what happened to Bobby? You two were so close."

"He is my best friend, Ma, that's different. He and Chelsea are together. I think she's even pregnant."

"Oh." She pauses and adds, "Well, are you sure? I kind of wanted grandchildren."

Oh god, it's always about her. "I still have a womb—that might happen. Besides, you still have Amy, I'm sure she will give you *plenty* of grandkids."

"Hey, there is no need to be rude now."

"Look, I thought you should know. Before you planned my whole marriage and life thing in your head."

She drives for a while all quiet and taps her right finger on the steering wheel. Tapping away her dreams, I suppose. I am relieved. She didn't freak out. I am still in the car. And there it is: the perfect photograph. "Mom! Stop the car!"

She slams on the brakes and skids a little on the road, forever leaving a mark of our changed lives. "What is it?" she asks, frightened.

"Oh, I just want to take a picture of that old falling-down farmhouse."

"What?"

"Over there! See it?"

She slowly turns to the northwest and says dreamily, "Oh yeah, and hey look, there is the Qu'Appelle Valley behind it in the distance."

I could see some rolling ridges that are interrupting the ongoing clouds. Finally, some break in the horizon. "Okay, cool, that will be in there, too."

I step out and see that she parked beside a never-ending road to the east and I decide to take a quick photo of that lonesome road as well. It is astoundingly straight. Something I am not. I walk around the car and feel something bounce off my leg. I look down and see a large grasshopper. He looks at me and moves on. I walk and feel another bump. I look at the road and see that there are many grasshoppers. Tonnes, in fact, and there seems to be one for every friggin' square foot of the road. Okay, just have to get this shot.

The farmhouse must be one hundred years old. It is grey and the roof is sunk in the middle. The sky is partly covered in puffy clouds, but it is still sunny, and the grass is brightly golden and green closer to the road. The rolling hills in the background are darker and give context to my field of grass. I aim and click.

The peaceful silence is broken by, "Are you going to stand there forever?"

Ever practical she is. I'm taking too long on a lonesome highway. Let's not enjoy the view for a moment or two. I turn around and remember the bugs on the road. "Hey, close your window, there are a tonne of grasshoppers out here."

"What?"

"Just close your window."

She is practically leaning halfway out of the car. I know that she can hear me. There is no other noise to drown me out. I begin to run across the road because the creepies are creeping me out now. I open and close the door quickly.

"Did you see that? There are grasshoppers everywhere!"

She laughs a little nervously. And then we hear a thud behind us. There is something in the car and it is behind my mother's head. I turn and see the largest grasshopper in my life hanging on to the side of the car above the back window. "There's a grasshopper in here! It's behind your head!"

"What? Where?"

My mother hates bugs. Especially big ones.

"Look, behind you! God, didn't you hear it hit the ceiling?"

She leans forward and looks back. "Oh. My. God," she says.

"It's okay. I'll get it," I tell her more bravely than I feel.

"No, it's in my car, I'll get it. I'm your mother. I'm supposed to take care of *you*, remember."

I can't argue with that. It is her job.

She grabs ten tissues and opens the door. By this time she is breathing through her nose like a stamping bull, and she stands up, turns around, and slams into that grasshopper like a young hunter all reckless but full of vigour. She throws the tissues down on the ground harder than the lightness will allow it to fall and she jumps back into the car in five seconds flat. We look at each other and start to laugh. We laugh so hard our eyes tear and our sides hurt. I look up and scream and she looks up and laughs harder. There is a grasshopper on our windshield outside of our car.

"Holee, there's his mother!" I say.

We laugh together and she pulls out onto the road again. We reach the Qu'Appelle Valley and park the car by some picnic benches. The wind is blowing her long hair into her eyes as she tells me that some young Native lover lost his girl and she called out to him when he was on this lake. I was nodding and watching the ducks eat the grasshoppers off of the grill of her car. I knew she would be alright.

Janet McAdams

The Door of the Devil

"I can't dance," Neva said, but the liaison officer was already pulling her to her feet and dragging her out onto the dance floor. "I don't want to," she laughed a little. Really, she said.

It was as if he didn't hear her. His breath was yeasty and wafted past her left ear. She felt first his belt buckle pressing into her as they circled the room. He spun her so hard her feet left the floor. The lights zigzagged crazily. She felt dizzier and dizzier, knew that if he were to let her go, she would fall, fall at the feet of the women who moved perfectly on their stiletto-heeled sandals, the men who could have taught classes in the states.

In the few months she'd lived here, she'd never danced. She always watched. Coatepequens danced before they could read. They danced in complicated, intricate patterns. She hadn't danced once since she came here, not once in all the evenings she'd spent at Mario's with her house-mates. She knew she could never chance it: letting her clunky North American movements loose among people who danced as if it were as simple as lying down for a nap.

The room was a blur of color and faces. She saw Kira's azure blouse and the bright orange drink she was holding. The room was hot and moist. Among the lights bouncing in the wall-sized mirror, she locked eyes with her own eyes. When the liaison officer whirled her by the mirror the next time, she saw herself again, her face over his uniformed shoulder.

When the music began to wind down, the liaison officer slowed them to a halt. She felt dizzy, breathless. His fingers were locked around her left wrist. "I have to go to the bathroom," she told him, but as the first few beats came over the staticky speakers, he began pacing in the two-two step of the Bancha. She pulled against his fingers, feeling them pinch the tender skin on the underside of her wrist. Something wild rose in her and she pinched back, twisting the flesh between her fingers, wanting to feel it between her teeth.

The liaison officer let go of Neva's wrist and stumbled a few steps backward. He looked puzzled. She edged away from the dance floor, her back cool in the spot where he had pressed his damp palm into her.

Neva took her seat across from Kira, who raised her eyebrows at Neva but said nothing when Neva looked away. Linda, one of the teachers at the American School, joined their table. "That girl was hiding guns. Mark told me," she spoke in a low conspiratorial voice, setting down a tall sweating glass and planting herself crosswise in the only empty chair.

"Oh for god's sakes, Linda," Kira said. "Mark's a fucking military advisor." She pronounced "fucking" with a hard g.

Linda sniffed, offended. Deb put a hand on her forearm. "Linda, Allison Lohmann worked for the church. She was raped and tortured before they killed her."

Linda ignored Deb. She pulled her arm away.

"Your boyfriend get bawled out by the State Department?" Kira sipped her gin and tonic. "So now everybody's a terrorist?"

Linda had no politics. Her desire to share this piece of information, that the social worker killed nearly two years ago had been working for the left, was to exhibit how in the know she was since she'd started sleeping with one of the American advisors to the First Army. The State Department had ordered an investigation and the tribunal was expected to rule next week.

Lawrence called it the *I'm-in-the-know* disease, every expatriate eager to share the latest, but the Americans were the worst. Neva wondered why Lawrence hadn't come tonight. He didn't seem to have any politics, left or right, but a ruthless will to uncover, dissect, analyze. Left or right—every player and act was subjected to Lawrence's cutting analysis. Neva was closer to Lawrence than to anyone else in Coatepeque, tempted occasionally to tell him about her other life in the States, the marriage she'd gone missing from all those months ago. It was a story he would find interesting rather than tragic. But she kept quiet while he sliced through layer after layer, dissecting the same friends he drank with and bummed rides and cigarettes from.

She still wasn't used to it. At home, people in the news were *in* the news. Here, no one was ever killed or elected to office without someone in the room being related to him, or claiming to be.

Linda and Kira were in a mutual pout, Kira glaring and Linda fiddling with her appearance, winding a blond lock around an index finger, scraping smudged eyeliner away with a long red fingernail. Neva had never been able to figure out if Linda was smart. Linda knew things. Not incountry things—every gringo who paid attention knew what every other gringo did about Coatepequen politics. But things. Facts. She rattled off information like no one Neva had ever met. That Peary's toes had snapped off on the way to the pole. That vitamin E and iron shouldn't be taken at the same time. That there were stars astronomers called white dwarfs. Facts and occasional comments about the size of her own large breasts were Linda's two main contributions to any conversation.

They hit the floor as the shot resounded through the room, a *crack!* so loud, the disco music became a pale backdrop behind it. A pair of traveling students, recognizable by their backpacks and jeans, were the only people in the room still standing. They must've felt themselves grow suddenly tall, trees on the edge of a clearcut through the forest. And then, sheepishly, they hunkered down.

"What the hell," Linda whispered.

"Shhhh," Kira put a finger to her lips and they waited in silence. They could hear a woman sobbing on the other side of the bar. On the floor beneath their table kernels of popcorn were scattered among the hair, fingernails, and grit. The underside of the table was thick with chewing gum.

The single shot was strange. A quick volley from an automatic rifle was not unusual, common enough at parties anyway, when an experienced guard accidentally discharged his weapon. Nothing surprising in a country where everyone was armed. Well, *she* wasn't armed. Of course, the guard in the doorway checked all handguns when people entered the Brit Club. But if everyone at her table had a pistol stowed somewhere it wouldn't have surprised her. No one wanted to hand theirs over. Guns disappeared here, like everything else. Besides, anything could happen. You might need your gun.

Slowly, people emerged from under tables and began to whisper and talk in low voices. Linda drifted away and then returned. "A marine shot himself," she said.

It was late when they left, nearly two. They had waited, until the police let them leave without questioning them. The students had followed them out into the foyer.

"Is there a bus stop near here?" one of them asked.

Deb shook her head. "It's hours past curfew. The buses stopped running at ten."

"How much for a cab?" The student was very tall. He carried a green North Face backpack over one shoulder.

"I don't think so," Deb said. "They don't run after curfew."

"Well, how are you getting home?" he asked.

Deb looked at Neva and Kira. "I guess we're walking." She turned back to the students. "I think you should come with us, crash in our living room. It won't be very comfortable. But the buses will be running at six and it's nearly two now."

The tall student argued with her, "It's not that far to our hotel, only a couple of miles. Jeez, we can walk that far."

Kira let out her breath in a little contemptuous burst and rolled her eyes at Neva.

Neva shook her head at the boy, and Deb said, "It's after curfew. You can't walk around downtown—you'll be picked up."

He was a foot taller than Deb. "Right," he said, "but we won't get picked up walking to your house." The redheaded boy put his hand on his friend's arm, "Jeff. . . ," he started to say.

"It's pretty quiet this time of night."

Just leave them, Neva thought. For chrissakes. "They don't pick people up in our neighborhood—," she started to say.

"Jeff, let's just go with them," the redheaded boy pleaded. "They live here."

"You can do what you want," Jeff said. "I'm going back to the hotel." He looked puzzled, unsure which direction to head for.

"Listen to me," Deb said to the redhead. "What is your name?"

"Patrick," he said.

"Listen, Patrick. The guardia cruises downtown all night because that's where the university is. He will get picked up, and whatever happens, he won't like it. Talk to your friend."

The other student looked Indian. She wondered if he could be from Oklahoma. He pushed his wire glasses into place and said nothing. Patrick, the redheaded student, was talking in a low voice to Jeff. Neva heard him say, *Please.*

"All right," Jeff said. "Which way?"

Neva did not realize how drunk she was until they left the Brit Club; she felt it sharply when they stepped out into the cool clear mountain night. She could never get used to the night sky here. In Oklahoma, the summers were so humid the air hung thick and cloudy between the stars and anyone on the ground.

In this country, she drank too much. Out with her housemates—who almost never drank and Deb not at all—she knew she could count on them to take care of her, make sure she went home, went home alone, usually anyway. She drank more than she had ever dared in the past. Every Friday and Saturday night, feeling the week's knot releasing, as she drank first beer, and then the drinks they made here from fresh pineapple and mango juice, mixed with tequila or rum. She would feel it dissolve, think: one more week under my belt, one more week undiscovered. Time was a kind of distance, and distance was safety.

They had not even been questioned, had been allowed to leave even before the ambassador had arrived. The body lay on the floor covered with a tablecloth, red haloed on the white cloth like a beautiful poppy. Linda said he was one of the embassy guards.

"The walk will sober her up," she heard Kira tell Deb and felt a brief edge of resentment tighten in her chest. It was a mile and a half to their house, mostly downhill, but she felt hungrier and hungrier as the sugary drinks wore off and hoped they would pass an open pupusa stand, sure the cortido and hot salsa would clear her head, would take the sweet sickly taste out of her mouth. But it was late, dead quiet, a ridiculous time, really, to be out in a country at war. They took chances now they would never have considered six months ago, as they grew blasé, as the war arced out into the countryside and away from the capital.

They walked a half mile or so without speaking. Neva felt flushed and out of breath, her skin damp from the heat and the walking. She realized that Deb was walking a few steps apart from them and turned to look at her, then turned in the direction of Deb's gaze at the carrier driving in their direction and slowing as it neared. She knew from Deb's face that she had been watching the truck a long time before it ever reached them. She knew, too, that Deb, who was almost never afraid, was afraid. She knew it from the way Deb's fingers wrapped tightly around her arm just above the elbow. Neva told her in a low voice, "I'm sober now," and she was, and Deb knew it, too.

"They're presidential guards," Deb whispered. "At least it's not the First Army." At her first embassy party, a pink-cheeked gringo looking to get laid had bragged to Neva that he was an advisor to the First Army. "And what do you advise them to do?" Neva asked, blinking at him in what she hoped was a naive rather than coy manner. He puffed up a little when he told her, "I tell them to kill commies," and she knew she was filing it away, a funny story to tell at the bar, funnier to tell back home except that no one there knew where she was or how to find her.

The guards were young, and that too was a good thing. When they shouted in Spanish, Deb released her arm and stepped forward. Neva could never follow Deb's rapid-fire vaguely Castilian Spanish. The accent sometimes worked against her, given Coatepeque's complicated class structure. Men of the oligarchy often greeted it with annoyance—for them, femaleness took precedence over everything, even nationality, here where to be American was everything. But the oligarchs had no use for gringa women who seemed uppity. These soldiers, though, were schoolboys, conscripted, she had no doubt, against their will.

And, heartbreakingly, against the wills of their mothers and sisters. The Saturday roundups in the small villages around the capital were terrifying.

Deb was talking to them in earnest now. Her voice was calm but as she spoke, she fingered the hem of her blue skirt. She smiled and shook her head, "Ay no!" she said, laughing. Neva felt Kira's breath on her shoulder even before she spoke: "What? What are they saying?" Neva strained to listen, inferring vaguely that the soldiers thought they needed an escort home.

"Oh great," Kira said, "it's after curfew. No one will know if we don't get home."

"Kira," Neva said, "you know we're safe. You know they don't touch Americans, not after the Peace Corps workers were killed. Not the right— they can't touch us." When the three workers had disappeared—a young man and woman from the States and a man from the Canadian Amnesty International—the United States had almost cut off all military and civil aid to Coatepeque. American aid now constituted more income for the country than the entire GNP.

"No, no es necessario," Deb said, lisping a little over the "c," the Castilian creeping into her accent the way it did when she was nervous.

And then several soldiers were climbing down from the truck, waving their guns a little, in the air mostly, as if to show that they were more friendly than not. One of them slid his hand under Deb's elbow and pushed her toward the truck. In his other hand, his rifle pointed toward the clear night sky.

The other soldiers had circled Neva and Kira, cutting them off from the three students. Deb turned back toward them, just before she climbed into the truck, and smiled stiffly as she said, "They say they want to give us a ride home. That it is not safe here. For women and foreigners. For us to be walking around."

Neva held back, shaking her head. The motion made her woozy. Deb took her arm. "Be quiet," she said. "Get in the truck. If we argue anymore, they may get mad. They've been patrolling all night and they're punchy."

The back of the truck had two long benches running lengthwise under a canvas top. There were seven soldiers, and six of them clustered around Kira's blond hair and tall body. Her striking Americanness. The students were on the far side of Kira. The truck was so dark Neva forgot them after a while.

Neva rode in silence across from a thin soldier with a serious expression on his smooth, clean-shaven face. He watched her without speaking, without wavering in his gaze. Kira's shrill laugh cut through the truck. "No!" she shouted, still laughing. "De Des Moines. De estado de Iowa."

The air was stuffy, hot on her clammy face. Neva inched along the bench toward the open end of the truck. The serious soldier touched his rifle gracefully, and she froze, sat up straight, and planted her feet on the wooden floor. With every bump and jolt, the sickness was worse, pushing against her throat, rising through her body in wave after wave. She put her hand over her mouth and held the other up to the serious soldier, hoping he would recognize this as "stop, wait," and scooted the length of the bench to the back of the truck where she lifted the canvas flap and vomited onto the rapidly passing cobblestones. Bright, sticky red, like the half-dozen fruit drinks she had sucked down at the Brit Club, the vomit was a long, thin trail behind the truck, a Hansel and Gretel trail, just in case they were headed not for home, but for the witch's gingerbread house in the forest. At the thought of gingerbread, she caught back her hair, leaned out the back, and emptied the rest of her stomach.

The serious soldier was behind her now, with the back of her blouse twisted in his fist. As Neva leaned back into the truck, he released it, smoothing the cloth clumsily. He offered her a bandanna, and she wiped her mouth, and then he offered her his canteen, and she drank, a long, sweet swallow of water.

"Gracias," she said. She did not look at him. The truck lurched and water splashed the front of her blouse.

"English teacher?" he asked, but then the truck stopped completely and they were swept up, piling out the back to the roadside where a yellow combi sat with its hood up. Neva felt lightheaded and leaned against the side of the truck. It was very late, hours after curfew. She wondered if they would ever get home.

A young Indian couple sat beside the combi on bundles tied with string. Beside them, a basket of chickens rustled and fidgeted. The students—Jeff and Patrick—stood together. Patrick fidgeted. Jeff had his arms wrapped around his middle as if he were cold and stood a little to the side, shifting his weight from hip to hip.

She was not a brave person. This was something she had learned from living here. She knew what it was like to be hit. She didn't often think about the husband she had left behind in Atlanta, but she thought about him now. The two years she withstood his slaps and shoves and, finally, a death threat—that was not bravery, but a shutdown of sorts. When the part that gets afraid goes away.

Here, though, where fear was shared and not private, it was impossible to shut down, to send the fear away. She was uneasy, as the soldiers motioned all of them together. Uneasy and afraid, as the lieutenant began to argue with the men working on the combi.

She thought of Will, the Americans in Solidarity with the Frente de Coatepeque, the speakers, the talks, the parties. The night they had chanted "El Frente con El Frente." She had no idea what that meant anymore. The day she had taken Deb to the hospital to get her stitches out, the song had gone round and round in her head. They'd walked past the long row of beggars on crutches, mothers holding children missing an arm or a leg or an eye. Deb had seen the look on Neva's face and hustled her past them. She thought of factory workers, environmental poisoning, thalidomide. "Land mines," Deb said. "The Front leaves them all over the countryside."

Neva shook her head, and Deb said, "I know. And they're the good guys. Amnesty International's been after them for years. And they conscript the healthy ones."

"I thought the army did that," Neva said. They were in the building with its thick smell of antiseptic and overcooked food.

"Everybody does it," Deb said. "The campesinos get it from both sides."

And earthquakes. And a plot of land that will never grow enough. Stay and starve or go—move into the barrancas, the ghettos around the capital, or lie down finally, into the long wound of hunger that has always been your life.

They drank coffee that night at the solidarity meeting. Miriam's special blend with a touch of hazelnut, delicious coffee really, and there was real cream, and turbinado sugar from the co-op. Kevin brought his guitar and played a song he had learned in Nicaragua. He handed out mimeographed sheets of the words and they sang along. Will had insisted Neva learn Spanish. "I had two years in college," she'd told him, but he had been adamant, so when Kevin led the group through *estoy/estas/estan*, she recited along with everyone else. Will smiled and nodded at her across the circle.

That was the first night Will's anger had seemed beyond her control. Usually, she could sense the tension early enough to diffuse it, but that night, she had been preoccupied. During the music, Miriam's baby had begun to stir in the womb, and Miriam had taken Neva's hand and laid it on her belly, where she could feel the hard knob of an elbow or a heel pushing against Miriam's skin. The baby swam and kicked in motion with the music. She and Miriam had smiled at each other and said nothing.

Will was agitated before they got home, driving jerkily through town and rushing into the apartment ahead of Neva. She caught the door before it flew back in her face. She felt something inside her become solid and brittle.

"Why didn't you sing?" he demanded, as soon as she got in the door. "Everyone was singing. Why didn't you sing?" He paced a little.

Soothing time, she knew. She knew to say: My throat's been kind of scratchy. Or: I'm sorry. I was trying to figure out how to pronounce the words. She knew the rules. Last week, Will had said to her: "Why don't you do what you used to do? Make a joke or pull a face. Why do you let me get angry like this?"

But she was so tired. She shrugged. "I don't know."

And then it began. He was across the room before she could back away. Before she could find something else to say, some way to apologize. He slapped her twice across the face. It stung the way her hands would sting during slapping games in the neighborhood, two children facing each other, their hands together. She was always the youngest, the slowest, the last to pull her hands away.

But she knew better than to touch her face. She looked down at the floor, noticing for the first time that the gray carpet had a pattern to it.

"God," Will said, "I'm trying to do something good here. You really piss me off when you act like this."

The Indian student clutched her arm and whispered in English, "Say you know me. Say I am with you." He spoke with an accent, Coatepequen probably but certainly Central American. This was the first time she'd heard him speak. The faces of the two American students were pale against the ink blue night, and it was quiet on the deserted highway. He hooked his arm through hers and clutched her hand possessively. He was breathing hard and his face glistened with sweat. "Just say I am with you," he whispered.

"Why me?" Neva thought. She was not at all brave. She began to think, for the first time in months, of the way a fist feels on a body, how a fist feels on a face. Of what it is to joke with someone larger and more powerful, watching for a sign that he has either relented or grown more angry. She thought she could not know these things with a Coatepequen, would not know how to read these signs.

She thought that a rifle butt would hurt more than a fist. She thought: "I do not want to die in this country, on this dark road."

The lieutenant was before them. It would never work. She was too old, late twenties to his teens. "Con migo," she said, coughing as she spoke. "Mi novio."

And then, without warning, he was gone, slipped away into the darkness. The guards shouted, leaving the huddled group of passengers, and chased after him. One of them tripped, and his rifle discharged as it hit the ground. Neva felt the sharp sound through her body, saw Kira run her hands down her side looking for a wound, saw the young Indian couple huddle close to the ground.

Miraculously, the guards began to laugh. One of them bent down and helped the soldier up from the ground. "Puta," he said, brushing the gravel from his fatigues. He picked up his rifle. "Puta."

"Your novio seems to have abandoned you," the lieutenant said to Neva. She tried to smile at him, felt her lips catch on her dry teeth. She remembered hearing once that Miss America contestants put cold cream on their teeth to make their lips slide back gracefully into those toothy smiles. She had never been so thirsty. The lieutenant turned away, uninterested.

She was squeezed between the Indian couple and the serious soldier on the ride back to town. Across from her Kira and Deb leaned against each other. "That was so fucking stupid," Kira said. "What the hell did you think you were doing?"

"Shut up, Kira," Deb said. "Just shut the fuck up."

The wooden bench was hard beneath Neva's bony rear. Under the canvas flaps, Neva could see one small square of the night sky. She thought she saw a movement across one of the fields and wondered if it could be the boy, still fleeing whatever this week's danger was. She watched the stars receding, trying to pick out the constellations from her childhood, but here, at this altitude, the sky was unrecognizable, the stars impossibly large and bright, so close they frightened her. The moon was a slender crescent and would disappear in a day or two. Its sharp edge pointed down into the gap between Mt. Xtapel and Mt. Pipile, the place they called the Door of the Devil.

Dan Taulapapa McMullin

Jerry, Sheree, and the Eel

Jerry always stayed in the kitchen
that's what fags in American Samoa do
take care of the young
the old, haunt the kitchen, cooking
and washing dishes. Anyway,
one usually saw Jerry
at the kitchen sink.
Now, this part of the story I made up:
One day
a missionary gave Jerry an eel to cook
but Jerry knew it was a sacred eel
and was taken by it.
He kept it in a rain barrel filled with water
as a pet. A sacred pet.
This other part's real again:
Every once in a while
Jerry put on a bright frock
beat her face and caught a taxi to town.
Pago Pago!
As Sheree she went to all the clubs
and asked all the straight boys to dance
because she only danced with straight boys.
And of course they all did
because you know

it's impolite to a person's entire family
to say, No.
Meanwhile
the sacred eel
grew larger and larger,
until its head was the size of a coconut.
Sheree, screaming,
made a pond to hold it.
This part's true:
One day
Sheree decided to form her own club with all the fa'afafine on the
    island.
They called themselves the Daughters of Samoa.
Sheree grew her hair long,
dyed it red
and got a job as Executive Secretary to the President of American
    Samoa Community College,
which she runs to this day.
And the ending I made up:
One night
the sacred eel grew so large
(as tall as a coconut tree)
that it chased Sheree
from village
to village
through
all
of
Sa
Moa.

Daniel David Moses

Gray's Sea Change

for Robert

Go off on your own, they instructed you. *Turn away from each
other. By talking to no one, you will learn the essence of*

communication. One among many young men and women
in training, you were willing to follow directions—your own

had yet to unfold—into the November chilly country
out near Nanaimo, willing, till one rock by the bay stopped you.

Did it hold itself up, hold itself out like a hand to you?
Is that how you knew you'd fit? Did it say, *Come to rest. Welcome.*

Let your wandering cease—? Did the ocean, its faces turning
up against that shore, also reflect the face of your solitude? Is

that why all the love of water you embraced after sixteen
summers swelled up too, a tide that carried you into the hands

of the waves? How cold they were—even through clothes. Your breath
    leapt up
like a fish but in a cry so vulgar, your neighbour, a young

woman guarding both a rock and a silence of her own, broke
out in laughter. Later she said the blur you'd been, a bobbing

head and twitching underwater limbs, had made her fear, just that
moment before, an octopus reaching out for her. Your curse

143

and less than graceful progress back onto the land transformed you
into a mere man. Not even a merman. Dry, almost warm

again in your clean, pressed jeans and sweater—though the memory
of your own thrashing through seaweed tentacles, your hard
　　scrambling

up rocks, your escape, still stung you like salt. The undertow had
almost sucked your running shoes off, had licked a shivering so

deep into your pores, you knew you'd begun an unfolding there.
Yes, as you cruised down, blue webs would soon have stretched
　　between your toes.

She told you how a sea lion had risen up out in the bay
after you'd gone, how directionless he'd been and slow. *Oh,* you

wondered, *Was he looking for me?* And now you're wondering too
if he might have made wet love to you, had you stayed there and
　　changed.

James Thomas Stevens

Regent's Canal

That our surface tension, our iridescence,
requires remaining fluid,
we never stray far

from the canal, the lake, the lock, the fountain, the floodgate,
the waterfall.

Where the arched iron bridge reflected
can watch elliptically on.

Herded with holiday strangers
into stalls
        at the Stables Market.

Surrounded by teacups
and cracked porcelain menageries.

Nothing I desire, but desire.

I think how many fetlocks,
here, set and mended.
A horse hospital not
            where I expected us to be.

Not surrounded by the sweet scent of curries
and incense, nor so saturated with experience
that I need to lie down.

Till startled by your arm against mine,
I rear and turn in my stall.

London, your bestiary of buildings unexpected.

Horses in your palace yards. Doves in the Orangerie.
Parrots in your marketplace and foxes in your fields.

Nights spent in a glasshouse
                                        overlooking the chalk farm.
Surrounded by white furs
and black rubber plumage.

On the streets below
the plume, not plume, but shock of blue
hair and bangles. Oxen of the modern,
they fit their own noses with rings.
Cyberdogs nipping
                  them urgingly into the future.

And bound in wools, we walk the markets, buying
silks and stone bracelets to fulfill our yulish duties.

And it happens unexpectedly,
the inevitable collision
                        on crossing Camden High Street.

A boy hawking toys and childhood delights
looses a monstrous sphere upon the air above our heads.

Together, inverted, we reflect on its quivering skin.

A bubble
descends and brushing your whiskered jaw

. . . bursts.

Kim Shuck

Absorbing Light

The mirror can still surprise me.
Some random dysphoric event and
I'm back in that small locked room.
Three days out of five some of the
X chromosomes switch off.
On the others there is too much information.
It takes planning.
I have to make sure I've washed
The right laundry.
The afternoon finds me absorbing light.
Sandpaper, lacquer
Removing and replacing the surface entirely.
The evening could find me
Dragging a cannon 300 miles through snow.
I might force a surrender.
This thing the mirror says I am or not, random in the day
So underdefined
No geometric proof, surely.
Times I stand so close to
Something like your answer.
A sweet, I hope to present you eventually.

Dan Taulapapa McMullin

A Drag Queen Named Pipi

Shoulder to shoulder
My sisters and I
Holding our heads high
File through the bone bar
Passing the hollow beds
Don't fall in!
We're just here to steal wreaths
To share with the living
Don't mind us
Don't fall in, we whisper
We'd follow you
Your guest is as good as mine
Single file dance into the bone bar
Meeting your sons after shutdown
When the real girls go home
When police close the other bars
To join us and the moon in her gray yard
Singing at last at the bone bar
Hunted by dogs, your sons
Our babies
Between silk orchids
In starlight

Daniel Heath Justice

Ander's Awakening

I.

*The fire spiralled past the delicate threshold of taut and tender flesh, cresting
at his skin, licking down his arms, legs, and belly, the longed-for burn like a
heady whirlwind through his senses, a dizzy mingling of pain and ecstasy.
The fire's return filled him with hunger, and dread, and he felt something
come loose in the innermost folds of his being, an awareness barely perceived
before, but which called, softly but insistently, to his awakening self. The
voice would grow louder—even now it was more urgent, begging him to sur-
render, to set it free. It was inevitable—his resistance was only delaying what
must—should—be.*

And he would change when the fire consumed him completely. Every-
thing *would change.*

*There was no fear . . . only hesitation, like the moment of uncertainty
before leaping from a cliff into deep and turbulent waters below. He inched
forward, tensing for the fall, when there came a shudder, then a tremor—a
presence from beyond, an intruder from the waking world. The fire drew
back, down into the marrow of his deepest being. The voice in that inner
place grew fainter, desperate to be understood but too weak to resist the pull
of his dawning awareness. It retreated, waiting.*

*The fire would take him again. And as much as he hesitated, he longed
for its return. It would not be long denied . . . .*

"Ander, I'll not warn you again." After numerous shouts and mumbled
curses, Uncle Guram's voice had at last gone soft, and this shift in tone—

more than all the earlier raging threats from downstairs—caused the bedding to rustle, and the youth's bleary green eyes to peep over the threadworn quilt. As the dream receded and the unwelcome waking world became real, he wondered if he'd again misjudged his uncle's patience. But he was alone in the garret; his uncle was still downstairs, so there would likely be no thrashing. Not this morning.

"I'm awake," Ander called out, teeth clenched from the sudden chill of his sweat-soaked nightshirt, pulling the bedclothes tighter as he watched the fog of his breath hang in the pallid light. Though there were no windows in the narrow chamber to let in honest air and give access to the sun and stars, there was enough light creeping through dozens of gaps in the wainscot to indict the room's deficiencies.

Aside from the rickety bed, a battered pine-board chest, and a cracked thunderpot, the room was an empty and unwelcoming place that had sheltered Ander for far longer than he wanted to remember. It was where his creaking bed squatted; it was where the few possessions of his past life lay piled among rank, rumpled woollens, crumpled strips of smudged paper, and the powdered remains of dried spring blossoms; it was where, every night, he quickly washed his delicates with frigid water, brushed the inevitable tangles from his proud tresses, and offered a few whispered words of doubtful praise to the Ancestrals, rather than the arrogant Dreyd of his uncle's insistent prayers.

It was the place where every long night ended, and where every long day began.

But it was not his home.

He took a deep breath, coughed in the cold air, and pulled himself up, cringing as his toes hit the icy floorboards. He was still a bit disoriented, and cold to the marrow; it was a few more moments before he could bring himself to lay the soles down as well, but knowing how far he had already strained his uncle's thin patience, Ander finally slipped out of bed and over to the trunk, where he replaced the unhelpful quilt with a thick pair of frigid woollen hose, grey breeches, and the rest of his clerking uniform, until at last he slid his already clenching toes into heavy leather boots, tried to smooth the wrinkles from his ink-stained waistcoat, quickly wove his sleep-gnarled hair into a quick, sloppy braid that fully exposed the two fleshy protrusions at his temple, and clomped down the stairs to face his uncle and family.

As he stepped into the light and welcome warmth of the common room, Ander heard his uncle mention that he would be home late that evening, as it was the night of the weekly Assembly, an undoubtedly tiresome meeting of the proud and moneyed leading Men of Jawbone Crossing who grappled with one another's ambitions, both great and petty. The others didn't respond to the pronouncement, being too focused on starting their meal of cold beef, porridge, and cups of *moché*.

All of this meant, to Ander's sudden and unexpected joy, that he'd missed the morning's Dreyd-chant. Finding strength to face the day in this household was hard enough upon waking, but standing through the endless litany of Dreyd prohibitions and exhortations on an empty stomach was almost beyond endurance. Lorrodrig, the fastidious old shopkeeper to whom he was now apprenticed, was no lover of the killjoy Dreyd, so there'd be no midday chants to endure, and with Guram otherwise occupied this evening, Ander would miss all but the Twilight Call. He didn't dare grin, but the gloom that had settled over his spirit from last night's disturbances had now nearly dissipated. Avoiding the Dawn Call was no doubt a little thing, but he relished every victory, no matter how small.

Shedree, his uncle's wife, ignored him as she spooned porridge into bowls. This was good; given the depth of her spite, anything that stilled her sharp tongue was welcome, as she was usually the first to offer a caustic greeting in the morning. The twins, Dree and Maller, were whining and accusing each other of misdeeds with their usual loud vigour, though Maller was distinguished this day by a particularly thick stream of snot-thickened tears running down his chin. Ander disliked the twins on principle, but they were young and entirely self-absorbed in their misery; he doubted they even knew his name or considered him as anything other than another fixture in the household, like a chair or a tin cup.

It was the older cousins—fifteen-year-old Win and fourteen-year-old Baryd—who excelled at torment, with Ander their target of choice, and they practiced with such delight and patience that Ander had had few full nights of unbroken sleep in the full six years that he'd lived with the family, for fear of again waking to terrible pains of the most intimate nature.

But this morning, Win and Baryd were silent, not even extending a glare or snide comment. Uncle Guram had returned to quietly eating his porridge, so Ander sat down beside Dree and reached for a bowl.

"I understand," Guram said as his nephew began to eat, "that yesterday you shamed this family by involving yourself in a public brawl."

The delicate truce was over. Now Win sniggered and looked up, his face a mask of pure malevolence. Baryd grinned but wisely kept quiet.

Guram turned to Win. "This is not a matter of humour, boy. This is a matter of family honour. It is not appropriate that a member of a jurist's family be involved in such undignified behaviour." He addressed his nephew again. "What say you, Ander? Have you once more brought disgrace on this family?"

Ander heaved a deep sigh and stared into his porridge. He knew an explanation would only cause him more trouble, but he also knew better than to risk Guram's wrath with a lie or an evasion, for no matter how oafish his uncle might look, with his brooding brows, ruddy bald head, and fleshy jowls, he was anything but a fool. "I didn't do anything wrong. I was defending myself."

"Defending himself, indeed! That's the rather thin wedge of the truth." Now Shedree's bitter voice joined the attack.

Ander dared a defiant glance her way. "It *is* the truth—they chased us to the river and threw stones, but we fought back. And they left us alone after that."

"And why by the worthy Dreyd would anyone have attacked you?" Guram's voice was smooth and level—dangerously so. A heavy silence came over the room. Even the twins went quiet.

"I . . . don't know, Uncle."

"I can tell you why, Ander Bandabee. But I suspect you already know." Now a thin smile played across Guram's lips. "Could it be that my troubled nephew—to whom I have shown extraordinary generosity these past years since his shiftless parents abandoned him to my patient care—could it be that my nephew has been seen by my friends and neighbours on the streets of this town, the very town that I have served honourably as elder and jurist for over twenty years. . . ." His voice was little more than a cold whisper. "That my nephew has been seen by the most dignified and respectable people in Jawbone Crossing in the disreputable company of mincing fops and low deviants, and wearing . . . *a Woman's dress?*" The last words came out in a hiss.

Feebly, Ander tried to explain. "It wasn't really a full dress, Uncle, just part of it. And we . . . well, really, it was just a bit of fun," he started, but his uncle's porridge bowl struck him full in the face, sending him sprawling backwards to the floor. As he clutched his mouth, pained sobs and bright blood bubbling through his fingers, Guram stood trembling above him, his features white with rage.

"A BIT OF FUN? FUN?" Guram's bellow shook the room. "It's not fun, you loathsome degenerate—it's abomination! You're a twisted, half-formed creature, you are, every bit your father's wretched seed!" A black boot caught Ander in the ribs, and the youth cried out again. "Look at you! Sitting upstairs mooning over your pretty hair like some girl-bride on her wedding night. Painting your face like a harlot—don't think I haven't seen the smudges around your eyes and lips when you come home after all decent people are abed. And I've also seen the glass baubles and the hose and all those laced unmentionables you keep hidden in that trunk of yours. You've abandoned what little grace your mother gave you, and you've made yourself into a disgusting, shameful spectacle, not even fit to be pissed on by dogs! Well, you'll not be darkening the good name and virtue of this household, not if I have to break every bone in your miserable body!"

He aimed another kick, but the blow never came. Instead, Guram knelt down and lay a heavy hand on his nephew's head, his fingers visibly recoiling from the two stunted sensory stalks that marked the youth's Unhuman ancestry. Grasping Ander's waist-long braid at the scalp, the Man wrenched him around, forcing the terrified boy to look into his eyes. "Understand me well: This is going to stop. The girl hair, the dresses, the whore paint—all of it. This is a Sanctified house, and it will remain so. You'll learn to be a respectable Man, or you'll be dead. I'll not be made a laughing-stock because my addled sister bedded some filthy Kynnish cur eighteen years ago. Now, clean yourself up and then off to the store with you, or you'll get another beating." Hauling Ander to his shaky feet, Guram pushed him toward the door.

"And nephew," the Man said pointedly, tossing Ander a kerchief, "if you don't cut that braid and wear your hair like a proper Man by your return tonight, I'll cut it for you before dawn. It must stop—it's your duty. Remember that *your* honour is *ours*. We are the only family you have, after all."

Ander turned slowly as he reached the threshold, his eyes burning with unshed tears of shame and pain and hatred. He held the kerchief for a moment before tossing it scornfully to the floorboards.

"Rot," he spat through bleeding lips, and slammed the door behind him. Then he turned and ran down the cobbled streets of Jawbone Crossing as fast as his trembling legs could take him.

II.

He ran until he was certain that Guram hadn't followed, then wound his way through the back alleys and unfenced yards. It was still early, and dark enough to keep his wounds from drawing too much attention. But he needed to find someplace to clean up before going to the Mercantile, for he couldn't appear for his clerking duties in such a sorry state. He didn't realize until he was almost there that he'd been heading toward the familiar side door of Quidd's Stablery.

It took a few moments for anyone to answer his insistent knock. As footsteps approached, Ander was gripped by sudden panic. What if it was Colonel Quidd who opened the door, or, worse yet, Sebur, the bullying stable-hand who'd only yesterday been part of the gang that attacked Ander and his friends? Neither Man liked the Strangeling, but only Sebur openly despised him. Ander wasn't ready to face him again, especially not like this.

But just as he was considering running away and hiding in the canopy of the cottonwoods down by the river until the swelling on his face went down, the door opened, and Pontepael Quidd stood there, never more welcome or more beautiful than at this moment.

And it was only then, safe at last in Pontie's strong and soothing arms, that Ander finally cried.

In a moment of exuberant storytelling just after arriving in Jawbone Crossing, young Ander had told his newfound acquaintances that his parents were off on another one of their wild adventures, leaving him with his maternal uncle for a short while until their fortunes were made and they could send for him to return to them in triumphant celebration. Yet in private and in public Guram countered—daily, it seemed—that his half-witted sister Zoola-Dawn and her wretched Kyn consort Walks-With-the-Winds had become criminals, burdening her dependable elder brother with a Strangeling child utterly ignorant of the Creeds and the Dreyd ways of Sanctity. They would never return, Guram insisted, but he would honour his family obligations by caring for their savage and unwanted brat.

The truth was somewhere in between, but he'd only told the full story to Pontepael, in a brief, unguarded moment a year past, after they'd first become lovers. In a teary whisper he told of the late-night raid on their caravan, the burning wagons and the ringing screams, the desperate flight to the false safety of the Crossing, and his parents' anguished departure before dawn, with no explanation of why they'd been attacked, nor why they had to flee without him. Later, Ander was filled with fear and regret—not for the love-bonding with handsome Pontepael, which was a welcome revelation, but for revealing an unhappy truth that he'd rather have kept close to his own heart. He knew too well from his vindictive cousins that secrets revealed could become merciless weapons.

But Pontie was as kind a friend as he was a lover. He'd been true to his word—he never told anyone, he never brought it up again, and he always turned the conversations when their friends or other age-mates would tease Ander about his parentage.

Ander didn't know if he was in love, but there was no one in the world he trusted more than Pontepael Quidd, the dashing, reckless son of the Crossing's favoured son, Colonel Parthid Quidd. The Colonel was the dauntless hero of the siege at Widley's Pike during the last of the Reachwarden's campaigns into the Lawless to the north. Some of that wild romance followed all his sons, especially the impetuous Pontepael, the third and youngest of his male heirs. Whereas Ander's Kyn lineage was the subject of sour gossip and pitying glares, Pontepael's ancestry was celebrated and codified in songs, stories, and traditions, and the good, Sanctified people of Jawbone Crossing had the utmost faith that their hero's line would continue with neither disgrace nor disruption.

At first, the boys' friendship was encouraged by their respective families: For Guram Bandabee, the pairing of his nephew with the son of the town's most respectable citizen strengthened his growing links with the old families of power; for Parthid Quidd, the match was a welcome and exotic diversion for his adventurous youngest, and their time together was time the Colonel could more fully devote to his older sons who would inherit the greater responsibilities of their estate. Yet rumours reached both homes about the less respectable activities of the constant companions and their various associates, and very soon Ander was apprenticed to old Lorrodrig from dawn until dark, while Pontepael was kept busy mucking out his father's stables and accompanying the Colonel on his surveys of stock and potential land purchases.

But the youths had many friends and many ways around the inconstant surveillance of their families. Pontepael rented some rooms in the top floor of the Welted Mallard, a dank and unpleasant tavern on the banks of the Hay River that catered to a wide range of appetites, asking no questions and offering no answers to gossips and rumour-mongers. Even Lorrodrig was a sympathetic conspirator, turning a blind eye to their furtive meetings during afternoon luncheon, provided that Ander worked twice as hard when he returned to his cataloguing. Ander never quite knew why prim old Lorrodrig had chosen to help them, but he suspected that his employer's overnight visits from a couple of barge-loaders twice a month made him sensitive to the young men's struggles.

They were careful, but apparently not careful enough. They'd been spotted leaving the Mallard early in the morning, arm-in-arm with a group of friendly fellows from the tavern. By whom, Ander wasn't sure, though he thought he'd spotted his cousin Baryd's pimple-scarred face earlier in the night. Certainly Sebur, the Colonel's devoted stable-hand and unofficial sneak, was among the Men who appeared out of the darkness screaming vile things and throwing rocks and other filth. Neither Ander nor Pontepael were averse to fighting back, as both were more than capable of defending themselves in a fair fight and had done so many times before, and the patrons of the Mallard tended to be a rather rough bunch, so what had started as an ambush with the expectation of an easy victory by Sebur and his gang became a rout, with Ander, Pontepael, and their new companions returning to the rooms above the Mallard to celebrate their success in their own special way.

But now, the day after that heady triumph, a much-diminished Ander Bandabee lay naked on Pontie's bed at the Stablery, his mouth so swollen he could barely speak, his face and ribs covered with blackening bruises and hardening welts, tears of mingled rage and gratitude streaming down his cheeks as Pontie gently bathed his wounds with a warm decoction of comfrey and mint.

Pontie had broad shoulders and a broad smile, dark eyes and thick, short-shorn black hair and long sideburns. He was two years Ander's senior, a skilled hunter, boatsman, and rider, a young Man loved and admired throughout the region, but here he was, tending so tenderly to hurts of this freakish, unwanted Strangeling. Why he wasted his time with such an outcast was beyond anything Ander could comprehend. Pontepael's kindness, his beauty, his perfection, made Ander weep even harder.

"Now there, sweets, you've got to hush. If my old dad or anyone else catches a whiff of you being here, we're both in for a thrashing, and you don't need another one." Pontie grinned as he softly lifted Ander's chin. "We don't want the other half of your face all bruised up to match, now do we?"

Ander took a ragged breath and shook his head.

"Good, then that's settled. No more tears, no more sniffles. You look rough, not a doubt about it, but that bruisewort soaking should keep your pretty brown skin from going too blue, and a day or two will bring the swelling down. No teeth broken, no stitching needed. Looks a lot worse than it is, though I reckon it feels worse yet. Now, we need to get you dressed and get you out of here before folks start looking for me."

Ander sat up and took Pontepael's hand in his own. "I couldn't think of anywhere else to go, Pontie. I didn't mean to risk . . ."

"Hold your tongue, sweets," Pontepael frowned. "Nowhere else you *should* have come, and that's certain." He sat on the bed and offered what he hoped was a comforting smile. "This is where you belong, sweets, right beside me, and no mistake, and it won't be long 'til we can do it on our terms. The time's coming. Didn't want to say anything before, but I've been putting aside some coins, building me a tidy sum, enough to set up a nice stable somewhere far from here. I'll need someone who knows books and can figure expenses and all that. Sure enough, everything's going to change. Just wait and see—all them dreams we talked about, well, they're going to be more than dreams soon enough."

Ander smiled, though with the swelling in his lips it looked more like a grimace. He reached over to the bedside table and took Pontepael's knife scabbard in his hand. "You could charm the green from the trees or the splash from the creek. I'm ready to go anytime you come for me. There's nothing keeping me here but you." He pursed his lips and reconsidered. "I have another year of service to Lorrodrig. He's been good to me, and I'm learning a lot about keeping books and buying and selling goods."

"That's fine. That's just what we'll need—a little more time for me to make the money, you to keep us on track, and both of us to spend it and have some fun along the way." Pontie reached over to stroke Ander's cheek with one hand, grabbing the scabbard with the other. "Don't you give another thought to those things your uncle said about you, sweets. He'll never know you, and that's his loss, not yours." His eyes grew hard. "But if he touches you again . . ."

Ander shook his head and pulled his braid over his shoulder, drawing it to its full auburn length in front of his chest. "Don't worry. If he does, you can have what remains after I'm finished with him. Now," his voice began to tremble again, and he turned his eyes to the wall, "do it quickly . . . please."

"You sure about this, sweets?"

"No, but I have to go back, don't I? I can't stay here tonight. Besides, it's better you do it than him."

Taking the braid in his hand, Pontepael sniffed and pulled the knife free. "It's a Dreyd-damned shame, it is. A Dreyd-damned shame."

III.

Though pedantic about the virtues of punctuality and decorous public presentation—among innumerable other details—Lorrodrig never mentioned his clerk's significant tardiness, nor did he bring attention to Ander's wounded face or ravaged tresses. A slight widening of the eyes and lifting of the brows were the only gestures that betrayed his concern. Yet Ander wasn't so deeply buried in his own misery that he failed to notice that there was no complaint about his quill-marks straying from one column to another in the accounting log, or his sloppy ink-drippings or visible piles of blotting paper, all of which would have ordinarily driven the merchant into a fussing fit.

Ander was grateful for the respite, especially this morning. Lorrodrig was a fair employer, but he was maddeningly fastidious about his store and its environs—nearly as much as his own velvet- and lace-draped self. The Man liked the surfaces in his spare back office clear of mess, with no papers, inkwells, quills, knives, or coal ash visible, just as he liked the whitewashed shelves in the front store to be free of dust and finger smudges, with all goods carefully organized according to their kind, and only a few of each item visible to avoid unnecessary clutter. Though he generally managed to keep his temper under control during the day, when customers bumbled around the store, knocking over bottles, shoving boxes to the back of the shelves, picking up items in one area and absently placing them on a different shelf, once the door was shut Lorrodrig would invariably descend into a cursing paroxysm of recriminations as he returned the store to its pristine state. While Ander was no stranger to profane language, he was always amazed and a bit in awe of Lorrodrig's expansive vocabulary, no doubt periodically enhanced by his barging friends.

Today, though, Ander revelled in the silent solitude of the back room. The merchant usually spent most of the day going through figures and accounting ledgers, often introducing Ander to yet another tiresome lesson in accountancy. But not today. Today Ander's duties were rather mindless—transcribing accounts from the front tally book to Lorrodrig's personal log in the back room—so he was able to drift into welcome memory without distraction.

"They're going to be more than dreams soon enough," Pontepael had said. Ander chanced a small smile, but flinched at the pain in his lip. They'd certainly dreamed a lot these past few months, more so as their families became increasingly intrusive. "I want to see beautiful things for a change," he had whispered to Pontie late one night, in the lingering moments before he slipped back through the shadows to his lonely garret prison. "I want to see beautiful buildings, beautiful vistas, beautiful people. I want . . . I want to *be* . . ."

He'd never finished the words, but Pontie knew his heart's desire, and they both knew it wouldn't be found in the backwater trading town of Jawbone Crossing, where life's predictable rhythms gave a firm and certain shape and order to those who lived there, where change was best avoided and difference worn down to more familiar forms. There was a given progression to things among the Crossing folk: You were what you'd been born to be, and you'd remain thus until you died, and stay that way in the memory of those who followed. Even a great hero like Colonel Quidd was, in the end, very much content with the role he'd been given, and he expected a similar satisfaction from his sons.

Ander's arrival had upset his uncle's place in this comfortable pattern, just as his mother's sudden departure over ten years before had brought the pall of shame over the Bandabee fortunes. The family had once thought that Zoola-Dawn's wild ways would grow calmer over the years, that the restless streams would find slower currents in which to travel. But on the very evening she was to be betrothed to one of the Narquish brothers, she ran off with a stranger—a *Kyn* stranger, at that—and supposedly married him according to his savage traditions. It was a heavy blow to the family, who had hoped to lift their fortunes through an advantageous marriage to the more respectable Narquishes, and a burdensome shame, to have one of their own bedding with little more than a beast. Ever the guardian of his family's honour, Guram set off after Zoola-Dawn's departure with a vow to drag her back by the hair if she refused to obey him and her duty, but he returned within the week bruised and bedraggled. He never spoke of what words had passed between them, but until the night she and her Kyn lover arrived with their strange issue, he'd never once said her name.

Ander didn't know why his theretofore-loving parents left him with a Man who so clearly despised them; he couldn't imagine what would have been so bad as to subject their only child to such a life. There was no love for him in the Bandabee household. They mocked his features—the strange, leaf-shaped ears and partial head-stalks that distinguished him fully from his Human kindred—and he returned their loathing tenfold. There was nothing but the thinnest thread of kinship that connected them. Where they were pale and burned easily in the sun, the rich bronze-brown of his skin only deepened in the summer; where their eyes were slate grey or pale blue, his were a shining green that sparkled with life, even when brimming with tears; the dirty blond hair of the females was pulled away and hidden beneath headscarves, while that of the males was chopped short at the nape of the neck and hidden by hats in public, but Ander's copper locks fell free to his back—or they had until that morning.

He was an odd, unwelcome thing that didn't belong here, as the Bandabees made clear every day and night. He wasn't a part of the natural rhythms of Jawbone Crossing, but it wasn't because he had a place elsewhere; he didn't seem to have a place anywhere. He was a wildflower unsuited for an ordered garden. No matter how much he hated them, he had no other place to go. So every night he'd suffer through whatever unpalatable meal Shedree had muddled together, make his way back to the cold room at the top of the stairs, and—when not slipping out to enjoy a furtive embrace with Pontie or spending the dark hours of the night fighting off his cousins' vicious amusements—surrender himself to dreams where he was loved, wanted, desired.

He was tired of being a Strangeling among Men.

He wanted to belong to someplace, to someone.

And most of all, above everything else, he wanted to know what it was to be—beautiful.

Tears burned at his eyes, and he hurriedly wiped them away as Lorrodrig entered the back room. The old Man clicked his tongue nervously. "Closing up, Ander. Best clear away your papers for the day."

Ander looked up, surprised. "Already?"

"Already? You've hardly moved for hours now." Lorrodrig hesitated. Tugging at a lace cuff, he gestured back to the front store. "You needn't go just yet—there's plenty of tidying to do, if you'd care to help me."

"Gladly," Ander nodded without hesitation, sweeping his papers, quills, and books into the top drawer of his desk, then added, noting Lorrodrig's flinch, "after I put these things back into their proper places, of course."

"Of course," Lorrodrig sighed as he spun on his heel and returned to the front, girding himself for the imminent campaign against chaos.

They worked until darkness, again in general silence, save for Lorrodrig's occasional sputter of disgust at the obnoxious placement of some small bag of cornmeal or a ceramic jar of pawpaw preserves. Ander had spent much of his time dragging items from the cellar to replace their sold counterparts, following that work with dusting—an endless battle, given that all of the Crossing's streets were packed dirt and crushed stone. Yet as the night began to deepen and the shelves were once again tidy and fully stocked, Ander decided to collect his things and leave for the night.

"You needn't go just yet, my boy," Lorrodrig called out from behind the long desk at the front, pulling at his sleeve. "Stay and have a bit of dinner with me for once. There's no hurry, surely—your uncle won't likely be at home on Assembly night." The Crossing's dignitaries were covetous Men who loved money and feared the Dreyd in equal measures, and thus Assembly was sacrosanct.

The old Man's manner was pleasant, but he seemed a bit uncomfortable— perhaps, thought Ander, because he'd never invited his clerk to share a meal with him before. Indeed, Lorrodrig had been a bit strange all day, much less given to peevish snarls than usual.

He considered the invitation. While not eager to remain in the shop, he certainly didn't want to go back to his uncle's home and face the leering grins of his cousins or Shedree's biting attempts at wit, and he didn't expect Pontie to be able to get free from his father's eye until later in the evening.

Besides, he *was* hungry.

"If you're sure you have enough. . . ."

Lorrodrig smiled, his long, crooked teeth making a rare appearance. "Of course, dear boy, of course—there's plenty for both of us!" He seemed almost relieved, and Ander suddenly felt an unexpected wave of empathy pass between them, for he suddenly realized that the merchant, too, had more than a passing familiarity with loneliness. Uncle Guram's snide comments about the unmarried old Man now made more sense—Lorrodrig's keen mercantile mind and fine trade goods were needed in the Crossing, but need wasn't love; indeed, it was barely tolerance. As was the case with the Bandabees, the finer families were more than happy to draw on Lorrodrig's skills to fill their homes with new fashions, foods, and gadgets from Chalimor and places even more exotic; they were even willing to trust their second sons or disgraced nephews to his training, so as to draw some measure of value from youths otherwise underfoot or expendable. But, to Ander's recollection, the old Man had never once been a guest in his uncle's home, or in the homes of any of the Assembly leaders.

As he watched Lorrodrig bustle about, bringing cheese, smoked ham, and wine from the cold cellar, pulling hard-crusted bread and currant jam from the shelves, Ander felt his eyes mist over. This, then, was the fate of the unwanted and unloved in Jawbone Crossing: to live alone, serving those who despised you and facing the scorn on their smug faces every day, finding comfort in furtive nights with shadow-draped lovers or a simple meal with a bruised and ragged young half-Man.

What a desolate life. And it was to be his as long as he stayed here.

Ander quickly brushed the tears away as Lorrodrig returned with a high-laden platter, but not fast enough to prevent the old Man from seeing his attempt at composure. Pursing his lips, Lorrodrig set the tray down and slid a pewter plate in front of his guest.

"The kettle is on; I'll bring the tea shortly. In the meantime, help yourself, my boy—there's plenty for all."

"All?"

"Yes," Lorrodrig nodded briskly, sitting down and pulling his sleeves back. "I've asked a friend to join us tonight, and he should be here shortly."

"Oh—maybe I should go. I don't want to be in the way," Ander said, sliding his chair back.

Lorrodrig shook his head and motioned for his guest to remain. "Nothing to fear, dear boy, I assure you. Indeed, you may well find this visit to be enlightening in many ways. I hope so." Seeing Ander's continued discomfort, Lorrodrig offered a comforting smile and delicately speared a chunk of white cheese from the platter. "Not all Men are like your unkind uncle, Ander; not all wish you harm. You can go whenever you'd like—I won't stop you. But I do hope you'll trust me, just a bit."

There was a knock at the back door, and Lorrodrig went into the other room to welcome his guest. Ander hesitated. He had no reason not to trust the old Man—though often cranky, Lorrodrig had never been cruel to him, or even particularly discourteous. But there was clearly more to the dinner invitation than a simple meal. His earlier sympathy toward his employer began to harden into suspicion, and his uncle's half-veiled accusations about Lorrodrig's interests in being surrounded by young men suddenly rang in his ears.

He looked up as Lorrodrig entered again. "He's bringing in a few items I'd asked him to collect for me from one of my warehouses," the merchant explained. "He'll join us in a moment."

Ander took a deep breath. "Why am I here?" he asked, his voice tinged with anger. "What is all this?"

Lorrodrig brushed a piece of stray lint from his velvet lapel. "Very well, Ander, very well. You have every reason to be hesitant, especially given this morning's misfortunes. But again, let me assure you that my intentions are pure, no matter what you may have heard from the caustic tongues of town gossips." Ander flushed, but Lorrodrig continued with an understanding shrug. "I've long been observing your rather unhappy domestic situation, dear boy, and thinking of ways to help. Yet it wasn't until today that my guest and I hit upon an ideal solution to your unfortunate problem. While the circumstances leading to this solution were quite unhappy, as attested by your current state, its timing is quite fortuitous. This very night offers us a chance to provide you with something that will change your life significantly, something that you've wanted for quite some time."

Confused but intrigued, Ander asked, "And what might that be?"

"Justice."

A new figure stood silhouetted against the doorway. "And freedom, sweets, freedom for us both." Pontepael walked over and set a large trunk on the floor at his lover's feet. As though unveiling a great treasure, Lorrodrig slowly opened the lid and gestured to his clerk to explore its contents.

Ander's green eyes went wide as he reached in. Confusion gave way to gradual understanding and then delightful certainty. And though his lips burned, he couldn't help but grin.

"Now, turn and take a look, sweets."

Ander hesitated. It was one thing to imagine this moment, to dream about it, but it was another thing entirely to face the distinct possibility that the reality would be woefully inferior to his imaginings.

He glanced at Pontie and Lorrodrig, who waited expectantly, sharing a strange and indecipherable expression. "Are you sure . . . ?"

Pontie nodded, still inscrutable.

Ander took a few deep breaths. His heart was hammering in his chest, and he could feel a trickle of sweat trail down his spine. Part of him wanted to flee, to escape this mad plan and these Men, to hide in his cold garret room and its unhappy familiarity. Everything would change tonight—everything. So much risk, so much uncertainty.

But they were risking themselves, too. He wasn't alone in taking this chance.

"Why?" he'd asked Lorrodrig when they started. "They'll know it was you—there's no way they won't know you helped me."

The old Man had nodded, wiping a thin-tipped brush on the towel draped over his arm. "Yes, of that there is no doubt."

"But why?" Ander had repeated.

"Perhaps because I was never brave enough when I was young. Perhaps, had I taken a few more chances in love and life in those days, I would be a very different Man today. Perhaps I would have someone to share this life with." He'd glanced at Ander's expression. "No pity, my boy—I have none for myself, and I refuse to accept yours. It is a simple fact, no more, no less. Suffice to say, I see something of myself in you, but at your age I was more concerned with my social position and making riches. It never occurred to me that I would want something simpler, something that you have in abundance."

"What is that?"

"Someone who loves you, foolish boy," Lorrodrig had chided. "I assume you don't need to ask why *he* is here, do you?"

Ander had looked to Pontepael then. The wide smile, the warm eyes, the scruffy goatee and tousled hair, the broad chest and tight muscles straining at the fabric of his tunic and breeches. Never had Pontie looked so handsome; never had he looked at Ander with more joy and pride.

And now, this lovely, loving Man wanted the Strangeling to look at himself.

Ander turned around slowly, as he was still finding it difficult to keep his balance. His head was still down, but he breathed in again and slowly raised his eyes.

This particular looking glass was a rarity in the Wilderlands; few families had more than a hand mirror, but with the fashions Lorrodrig ordered in from Chalimor and far Sarvannadad, he'd wisely decided to order a mirror that gave customers a full view of themselves. It had proven a lucrative decision, and was as popular among Men as among Women. As Lorrodrig was fond of noting, sometimes with particular relish in the presence of an Assembly member's wife, Men were even more given to vanity than Women—they simply lacked insight into their own conceit.

But it wasn't vanity that now took Ander's breath away, not entirely. It was a different kind of self-regard, a sudden recognition of something that had escaped his observation all his life. It wasn't the shimmering sheen of the jade gown split at the hip that dripped in soft folds to the floor, nor the matching, wide-brimmed hat trimmed with peacock feathers and bright glass beads that caught the flickering candlelight. It wasn't the tight, knee-high boots of dyed green leather, nor the delicately wrought rings, earrings, bangles, and necklace of copper and glass that complemented his tawny skin. Nor was it the trimmed auburn hair brushed into soft, full waves at his shoulders, the powder and skin paints, the eye-coal, the shaped brows and curled lashes, the lilac nails, the rich stain on his full lips. No bruises, no wounded flesh, no ravaged locks.

It wasn't vanity that made him quiver with suppressed sobs. It was a dream realized, all the more precious from the long-harboured fears of its impossibility.

His voice was weak. "I'm . . . I'm . . ."

From behind, Pontie slipped his arms around Ander's waist and whispered into his ear. "Yes, sweets—you're beautiful. But then, you always were to me. Now you can see it, too."

They stood in front of the looking glass for a long time, Ander leaning back against Pontie's chest, Pontie pulling him close. Lorrodrig's clearing throat shook them from their reverie, and they turned to him, faces aglow.

"He will need a name, of course. We can hardly just announce him as 'Ander Bandabee,' can we?" He was cleaning his brushes and returning the lids to the jars of skin paints and dyes, but he looked at the youths with every bit the joy of a proud father. "Let's play with the letters. Perhaps

'Danda' or 'Anderra'? It should be something easy to remember, but not so familiar that others will recognize him."

"Danda, maybe?" Ander said. He hadn't given much thought to another name. "That sounds nice enough."

"No," Pontie shook his head. "It don't fit, not at all."

He stepped back, crossed his arms, and surveyed Ander's image from boot to brim. Gradually he began to walk around the Strangeling, nibbling one thumbnail in contemplation, as the others watched him and waited expectantly.

"Ah, sweets, I have it," he announced at last, his face breaking into a broad grin. "Denarra. Denarra . . . Syrene. That's the name for my sweet and lovely lady."

Denarra Syrene. Ander felt a hot tremor pulse through his body, a rush of recognition as true and certain as the view in the looking glass. "Yes," he whispered. "That's my name. That's who I am."

"But what does it mean?" Lorrodrig asked. "Does it mean anything?"

"I don't know," Pontie laughed. "Probably not yet, but I'm sure he'll— *she'll*—make it mean something soon enough!"

The old Man nodded. "Well, then, if all is in order, it is time to go. Are you sure you are ready for this, Ander . . . Denarra?"

Turning to the mirror, the Strangeling looked again, taking strength from the confident figure who looked back with admiration. "Absolutely," Denarra said, her voice strong and certain. "Let's pay my dear uncle a visit, shall we?"

IV.

The Dreyd-fearing patriarchs of Jawbone Crossing didn't hold their weekly Assemblies at the brick Hall of Sanctification where they worshipped, but it had never occurred to Denarra why this was the case. Indeed, she'd never heard until this night precisely where the Assemblies took place. Such knowledge, while not secret, was unspoken—those who were supposed to know it, knew it; those who weren't, didn't. She doubted that Shedree or her bitter brood knew where Guram went every Assembly night; even if they had, Guram would never have invited commentary on the matter.

Jawbone Crossing wasn't a very big community—a few thousand people crowded on a spit of sand and stone between the Hay River and the rocky slopes of the High Hills—but there were certain areas that were clearly more respectable than others. For example, the Welted Mallard tavern where Pontepael kept their rooms was on the riverfront, a place with a decidedly lower reputation than the households of the finer families, including that of the ever-ambitious Bandabees, which hugged the High Hills as far away from the river as possible. The Hall of Sanctification stood squat and unforgiving on a narrow ridge above the town, reminding all in its dark shadow that the grim Dreyd were the new and unquestioned law of this world and those beyond.

The Assembly seemed to have missed that message, however, for the place where Lorrodrig and Pontepael were leading Denarra was well beyond the Hall's reaching shadow. Indeed, if not for the fact that the Men at her side had taken such care with her preparations, she would have thought they were playing a cruel prank, for the building that loomed before her was a decrepit-looking wharf house even farther down the river than the Welted Mallard, buried in the midst of a dozen similar buildings that she'd once thought abandoned to the wind and waters. But their nervousness was palpable, and even Denarra could feel a wrongness about the place—the same feeling she had when her uncle was near.

The building was made of the same black-red brick that formed most of the town, but worn and discoloured from the harsh winds that came from both the hills and the river at this end of the Crossing. There were no windows on either floor, just a broad, rust-reddened door on the far end with a single, red-glassed lantern swinging forlornly on a hook at its side. Refuse and coal slag littered the area around the building, adding to its general malaise of neglect. A ragged, half-starved cat slunk away when the trio drew near, but this was the only other living creature they encountered— not even a rat or a stray dog interrupted the silence of the night.

A chill, moist wind swirled around them, and Denarra shivered violently. Though beautiful, the silken dress offered less protection from the cold than her old woollens, and it would take her some time to get used to the difference. But she *would* get used to it, of that she was certain.

Pontie slipped his arm around her waist as they approached. Denarra realized that he, too, was trembling, but it wasn't just the cold—this was a terrible risk he was taking, in some ways much more dangerous and with much more devastating consequence than her own actions. She was just a half-breed Strangeling, after all; no one had high expectations of her behaviour. Pontie was the respected son of the Crossing's most beloved citizen. He was giving up a lot—as was Lorrodrig—to help her.

"Maybe we should go back," she whispered, as much to herself as to Pontie, as Lorrodrig made his way to the door.

He looked down. "Now, sweets, we already talked about this. We've got to go on."

"But your father—your inheritance . . ."

"Enough," Pontie said, his voice suddenly hard. "Do you think you're the only one who knows what it's like to feel a Man's boot in the ribs, who's got dreams and hopes and fears? This place is going to kill us both, sweets, if we don't get out, and I'm not staying just to collect a few more coins in my purse. I just want to be *me*, and if this is what it takes to be free, well, that's what it takes, even if I have to scrape and struggle for the rest of my days."

He shuddered again and took Denarra's hand. "I have to go on . . . and I want you to go with me. But either way, I'm going."

Lorrodrig stood at the door waiting for them, hands crossed over the handle of his walking stick, his impatience obvious even in the red lantern light. Denarra leaned up and kissed Pontepael's lips. "Lead on, my love," she whispered as the old Man opened the door and they followed him into the musty darkness.

The passage was dimly lit by foul tallow candles set on rough brass shelves jutting out in long intervals along the walls. Lorrodrig coughed and held a handkerchief to his face, but the stink of the oily smoke permeated the air, and his coughing continued unabated.

At last they reached another stout door, which Lorrodrig banged with the tip of his stick. After a long delay, an aged brass panel near the top of the door opened and a voice hissed, "*Why are we pure?*"

"*We are Sanctified,*" Lorrodrig replied, before coughing again.

A bolt slid away, and the door creaked open. Warm golden light and the heady scent of strange, sweet spices beckoned them forward down a long passage, away from the sour stink of the tallow lights.

Once they were out of the door-guard's hearing, Denarra whispered, "How did you know about this?"

The old Man's smile was bitter. "Husbands sometimes forget that their wives have brains and ears, and keen memories to match. Wives listen, and learn, and remember, and each of those Women is more than happy to share what they've learned with one another, forgetting in their turn that the shopkeeper sizing their fine new dresses or filling the order for their latest fashionable enthusiasm has ears that can hear as well. There's not much I don't know about the good people of Jawbone Crossing, my dear, not much at all."

Denarra didn't respond. She'd never given much thought to the scorn Guram and other Men in the Crossing had for the Women in their lives, and she certainly had nothing but resentment for her uncle's wife, the Woman with whom she had the most contact. It was hard to imagine She-dree as anything but a vindictive extension of Guram's will and motivation, but Lorrodrig's observation sparked a bit of sympathy in the Strangeling, who suddenly saw her own dissatisfaction with life in this place reflected in the Woman's pinched face and hard eyes. Denarra wasn't the only person in that household chafing from the constant ache of unrealized dreams.

Pontepael's arm tensed, breaking Denarra's reverie. They'd reached the end of the passage. A translucent gauze curtain separated them from the low hum of voices and glow beyond. "Are you ready, sweets?"

"As ready as I can be."

Lorrodrig reached forward and swept aside the curtain, motioning for his companions to step through.

It was the light that first captured Denarra's attention. The space they entered was the ground floor of a wide atrium stretching nearly the full length of the warehouse, with a wrought-iron balcony ringing the entire opening on the second floor. Bright lanterns of yellow glass stretched from long hooked poles in spaced increments along the balcony's edge. A gilded chandelier hung suspended from the ceiling, its diffuse light casting soft warmth throughout the room. The luxurious radiance of this place was so unlike the cold and grim Hall of Sanctification, so different from any place she'd ever seen in the Crossing and its Dreyd-determined drabness.

As her eyes slowly adjusted, she became aware of just how different this place was, for it was then that she noticed the many lovely Women draped in elaborate gowns and ropes of false jewels or revealed in various degrees of undress. Some lounged together on plush velvet sofas, idly snacking from dishes piled high on silver stands, while others reclined giggling on piles of gaudily coloured cushions on the carpeted floor and inhaled strange, sweet-smelling smoke from small braziers beside them. Others sat quietly at tables drinking various bright concoctions out of fluted pewter or blown-glass vessels.

And everywhere among these perfumed and painted Women were Jawbone Crossing's finest Men, each surrendering himself to his wildest whims and fancies. Here was Fardin Vetch, the city warden, lying on pillows between three naked bodies, his breeches around his knees, his eyes closed as he inhaled the vapours from a brazier and idly traced his fingers across his companions' flesh. Not far away from the warden stood Manto-meer Drash and his brother Hanit, farmers with the reputation of being among the most fervent in their dedication to the pleasure-hating tenets of the Dreyd, both roughly slavering over the bare chest of a young Woman whose eyes were filled with far more distaste than desire. Bartle Ambelard, the Crossing's printer and stationer, strolled leering up the stairs to the private rooms of the second floor with a Woman wearing nothing more than a wide-brimmed yellow hat and knee-high stockings. Among the respectable Men lingering on the first floor were the miller, a moneylender, two shipping merchants, and even a lesser Dreyd Purifier, one charged with purifying the ranks of the Dreydcaste of undesirables wrapped too tightly in the passions of the flesh.

"*This* is the Assembly?" she asked, her voice wavering in shock and growing disgust. "*These* are the good Men that my uncle praises so highly?"

"Yes," Lorrodrig replied. "This is the truth of it, my dear. And now you know." Sighing heavily, he walked back toward the door.

Pontepael squeezed her trembling hand. "We should go now, sweets. There's nothing more to see here."

"No, we can't go yet," Denarra shook her head as they moved through the atrium, her green eyes peering through the dizzying smoke, seeking out familiar faces, locking the images into her memory. Few in the small crowd paid them any attention, other than to cast appreciative glances at the lovely stranger on Pontepael Quidd's arm. "I have to see . . . I want to know if . . ." She stopped. Her body went rigid.

On a red velvet sofa in a far, shadowed corner of the chamber, flanked by a quartet of beautiful Women who in no way resembled Shedree's Dreyd-endorsed plainness, sprawled Guram Bandabee, his fat face red, his rubbery lips split in a lascivious grin. He was still clothed, but his vest and shirt were open, and his pale skin was beaded with sweat.

Pontepael pulled at Denarra's hand. "Let's go, love—you've seen what you needed to see."

Denarra ignored his entreaty, slipping her arm more firmly into his as she walked toward her uncle and his companions. Guram noted their arrival with a nod and a quizzical look that softened into a warm, fatherly smile as he recognized Colonel Quidd's youngest heir.

"Pontepael, my boy, what an unexpected pleasure! I didn't think your father would bring you here until you were a bit older." He hugged two of the Women closer to him.

"I'm nineteen summers now, sir," the young Man replied.

"Old enough to know a Man's true pleasures, eh?" Guram chortled, ignoring Pontepael's chilly tone and pulling himself upright to more thoroughly appraise his visitors. "And old enough to recognize rare beauty as well. Who is your companion? I haven't seen her here before."

Before Pontepael could speak, Denarra stepped forward and daintily extended her hand. "I'm new," she said, her voice low and breathy. "Denarra Syrene."

"Enchanted," Guram said, taking her hand and gently kissing it, stroking the soft underside of her palm. "Delighted to meet you." He turned back to Pontepael. "I didn't think you were the kind of Man to enjoy such delicate company. I obviously gave too much credence to the rumours about you and my ridiculous nephew. Ah, well, I'm glad to be wrong. You've chosen yourself a sweet morsel there, Pontepael. If you get tired of her, let me know. I may not have your energy, but experience has its merits."

"Yes, sir, I'll keep that in mind." Pontepael moved to leave, but Denarra remained in place, a strange smile playing across her lips.

"Experience, you say, sir?"

Guram leered at her, his hands idly stroking the breasts of the Women in each arm. "Intrigued, my pretty one?"

"Curious, more than anything," she said. "Illuminate me."

He laughed again. "You're a feisty little strumpet! Curiosity is a dangerous thing, pet—you may find yourself taking on more than you can handle. Such pleasures aren't for the weak or skittish, and you're very young, though you're certainly old enough to be educated by a Man who knows what he's doing."

"Yes, I am very young." Denarra's face was flushed and her eyes were bright in the strange light. "But you'll find that I know quite a bit about the ways of love, and even more about pain. Pontie has taught me about the former; his kindness has undone much of the damage from the lessons you've given me about the latter." Guram's grin wavered as Denarra wiped the facepaint from her cheek to expose a purplish bruise, then vanished entirely when she raised her hand to pull her hat back and brush the hair from her quivering sensory stalks.

The Man's eyes grew large, and his mouth went dry. "You!" he gasped.

The warm air flared hot. A sudden wind swept through the room, and the lanterns began to sway and then shatter from the unseen force, their burning contents spraying to the ground. The great chandelier swung back and forth as fire and smoke rose high in the air. There were screams and shouts, and the crowd surged toward the exit, pulling Lorrodrig away from his companions.

The Women at Guram's side fled, but the Man lay pinned to the sofa, unable to free himself from Denarra's unyielding gaze.

"All these years," she hissed, shaking off Pontepael's restraining hand. "All these years you've beaten me, cursed me, tried to crush every shred of beauty I cherished. All these years you said I was a shame on our family, a burden, a degenerate who would have been better dead than imposed on you and your vindictive brood. I've suffered through your cruelty and scorn, and I even sometimes believed you, because you and your world said in every way that I didn't belong. And now I find *this?!*"

The heat became stifling, and even Pontepael had to retreat as purple fire danced along Denarra's trembling flesh. Her clothes erupted into bright flame and smoke, and her auburn hair and head stalks wove back and forth in a pulsating rhythm. And as the strange fire surrounded her, Denarra's voice grew stronger, shaking the warehouse with its force.

"You're a lech, and a hypocrite. But worse, you're a liar, to yourself and the world. And I will no longer be wounded by your lies, Uncle. I'll live my truth, and the world will know yours as well."

There was a sudden sharp snap, followed by a booming crash as the chandelier collapsed, sending yellow flame roaring to the ceiling. The wooden beams groaned, cracked, then crumbled, and the entire warehouse collapsed inward, the roar of flame and wind drowning out the screams of the proud patrons and fallen Women who had found their way outside before the structure's immolation. They were joined by a growing crowd of townsfolk—wives and children, the low-born, unpropertied, or simply unpopular—who came to witness the consuming firestorm and the public humiliation of the once-proud Assembly members of Jawbone Crossing.

And from the crackling remnants of the warehouse, bathed in a lavender light, stepped two figures, pulling a third behind them. The first was a tousle-haired young Man, broad-shouldered and well-muscled, his soot-covered face beaming, his fine clothes ravaged by fire but offering no diminishment of his defiant bearing. The second was a young, auburn-haired Strangeling, naked save for the remnants of a gossamer curtain pulled tight across her now full breasts and round hips. More than the copper-brown skin or the slightly leaf-shaped ears, it was the four small sensory stalks—the four of a she-Kyn, two more than she'd had at birth—that revealed her Unhuman heritage to the world, a heritage that no longer filled her with shame. She walked with dignity beside her companion, barely giving thought to the heavy-set figure on the pallet behind them, a red-faced Man who muttered silently to himself as they dragged him out of the ruins and into the crowd. He stumbled to his feet, made a vicious gesture at the Strangeling and the young Man at her side, and shoved his way past the hooting and jeering townsfolk into the welcoming darkness beyond.

V.

Denarra awoke slowly, gradually surrendering to the bright light of morning. She had no idea how long she'd been sleeping, but she felt quite refreshed in spite of the events of the previous night. She reached beside her in the bed, but Pontepael was gone, probably downstairs helping Lorrodrig plan their imminent departure. The old Man's kindness was as unexpected as it was welcome; he'd offered the young couple his guest room when they left the remnants of the warehouse, as it was clear that there would be no welcome for them elsewhere in town. The sooner they left, the better, for them and for their benefactor, who risked much in harbouring them, even for one night.

She sat up and stretched, looking down in renewed amazement at the new changes in her body. New, certainly, but not strange—she felt more comfortable in this body than ever before. It would take some time to get used to the differences, to the curves and the folds, so unlike the rigid lines of the other flesh she'd known, but learning how this form functioned would be a pleasure, especially with Pontepael to share the journey.

Her old clothes were no longer practical, especially around the hip and chest, but Lorrodrig had kindly offered her two more dresses from his stock. Neither fit her particularly well, but silks were better than scratchy, smelly woollens. She dressed in a plain, sky-blue frock and simple white hose and doeskin boots, and brushed her hair as best she could—she now regretted cutting off the braid, as there wasn't much she could do at this length.

It took longer to dress than to pack. Aside from Lorrodrig's gifts, which she placed in a linen sack, there wasn't anything else to gather—what few belongings she'd had were back at her uncle's home, and he was welcome to them. It was a small price to pay for her freedom.

Smoothing out the bedclothes before departing, Denarra went down the stairs to the storeroom, where Lorrodrig sat with a cooling cup of tea as he went through the figures on his secondary accounting ledger. He looked up and nodded in acknowledgment as the Strangeling joined him.

"Good morning."

"Almost afternoon, more like it," he said, flipping a page. "The water's almost hot; shouldn't take long to boil."

"That's fine; I'm not too thirsty right now, anyway. And thank you—for everything."

Lorrodrig smiled as he smoothed the wrinkles from one of his sleeves. "Least I could do, my boy . . . er, my dear. I'll be warmed by the memory of those strutting birds all plucked and singed for the rest of my days. Not at all what I'd expected from your Assembly visit, but certainly well worth the inconvenience!"

Denarra laughed. It was a welcome sound, too often hidden in her earlier life. She resolved to do much more in the future. "I wonder how they'll explain things to their wives now!"

The Man's face darkened. "They've already found a ready explanation."

"Really? That was quick work."

"Yes, but effective. They claim it was witchery. And they blame you."

"Me?" Denarra was thunderstruck. "What about the brothel, the Women, all these Men with their clothes off . . . ?"

Lorrodrig sighed. "Don't underestimate the willingness of people to explain away unpleasant truths in order to retain the conventional and to keep change from making them question what they want to believe. You challenged all of the Crossing's most powerful leaders, revealed their hypocrisy to the world, humiliated them in the worst way possible. They aren't going to thank you for that, my fire-making friend."

The Strangeling slumped into a chair and dropped her head into her hands. "Then what was the point of all of this?"

"To live for honesty, damn the consequences. Whatever they say now, whatever they do, they'll have to live with the knowledge that other people know about their dishonesty. They won't be able to hide their true selves with any kind of confidence now. That's a victory, at least.

"Besides," he added, "you've found a truth in your own life that most people never know. You are very fortunate, Denarra Syrene, very fortunate indeed."

Denarra sighed. "I suppose. But I still would have liked for Guram to know what it is to be despised a bit longer."

"He'll know it. Remember, his position in this community has always been a bit uncertain; he wouldn't have fought so hard to be seen as respectable and responsible if he was confident in his reputation. This has set him back, to be sure. His association with the 'witch' who caused all the trouble doesn't help him much, either."

They shared a laugh as Denarra stoked the fire in the stove to prepare the kettle for her own tea. As the water began to boil, she asked, "Where did Pontie go?"

"To meet with his father."

The Strangeling froze. "Why?"

Lorrodrig reached over and patted Denarra's arm. "The Colonel sent a messenger requesting the meeting. They're at the public house, where there's little danger of his father making a scene. He should be back soon."

Still not comforted, but knowing that her appearance at the tavern would simply add more difficulties to what was no doubt a vexed conversation, Denarra resigned herself to waiting impatiently for Pontepael's return. And when, hours later, he did step through the door, his grim bearing made her even more nervous.

"We need to talk," he said, heading upstairs. She followed, casting a quick, frightened look back at Lorrodrig, who shook his head sadly.

She found Pontepael sitting on the edge of the bed, his hands balled into fists, his eyes focused on the plank flooring. Denarra lingered at the doorway until he looked up. He was crying.

"I . . . I can't go with you, sweets," he whispered, his voice cracking. "You've got to leave, but I can't go with you."

"What . . . why?"

"My dad . . . he'll kill you if I leave."

Denarra knelt between Pontepael's legs and took his face in her hands. "I'm not afraid of him, love."

"You should be." He grabbed her hands, and the hollow fear in his eyes filled her with palpable dread. "He's not the hero people here think he is. Do you know how he became so wealthy, made his fine reputation? He was a mercenary, selling his services to those who offered the most. And he didn't care what he did, who he worked for, as long as the fee was high. He just happened to be in a lucky place at the Widley's Pike siege—he didn't mean to be a hero, but he certainly knew an opportunity when he came across it."

"Who told you this?"

For a moment Pontepael couldn't speak. When he found his voice, he said, "My ma, before she died. She told me about what kind of person she'd married. I didn't believe her, not really, not until I saw some papers in his study. Slavery, theft, smuggling—he did it all."

"But that was a long time ago."

"Not long enough. There's nothing here holding me back; he knows that. He knows that the only thing to keep me here is my love for you. So that's what he's promised to destroy if I go."

Denarra pulled one hand away, and a flickering purple flame erupted in her palm. "Let him try. After last night . . ."

"We can't trust in that again, sweets. And I can't take that chance. I *won't*."

They were silent; there was nothing left to say. As the full import of his decision became real to them both, a wail forced its way out of Denarra's throat, and she collapsed into Pontepael's arms. He held her tightly, his own sobs shaking his broad frame. They clung to each other for a long time. At last Pontepael stood and pulled her close, his lips pressing hard against hers.

"We have a little while yet before you have to go," he whispered. "Let's make a memory that'll last until . . ."

"Until then," she smiled sadly, and lay back on the bed.

Lorrodrig had arranged for Denarra to travel later that night with his barge-working friends by river to Happenstance, a larger city to the northeast of the Crossing. There, he said, a Woman by the name of Mardisha Kathek was raising money for Unhuman charities; he'd heard that she had a particular interest in education for the disadvantaged, so he suggested that the Strangeling seek the Woman out. He was certain that, given her skills in reading and figures, as well as her sweet temperament, Denarra would no doubt make a good impression. She was less certain of the possibilities than he was, but was in no position to refuse what seemed to be the best available option.

"What about you?" she asked the old Man. "Aren't you going to leave, too?"

"No, my dear, I'm not."

"But it's not safe for you here."

He shrugged. "It's as safe as it ever was. They can't replace me yet; they need me. And I'm too old to start over. Adventure is for the young. But my prayers go with you, my dear, as do my hopes." He handed her a leather purse. She could hear coins clinking inside. "It's not much, but it'll help ease your journey for a while."

She flung her arms around him. "You're a darling, Lorrodrig, and a dear friend. Thank you."

He patted her back awkwardly before pulling free and smoothing the wrinkles from his vest. "Of course, of course. Take care, my dear. Be safe, and be true." He looked up the hill, where Pontepael stood beside his father, who sat mounted on a horse and watched to ensure that the Strangeling left and his son remained. "And don't doubt his love for you."

"I don't," she said, her eyes filling with tears. "I couldn't."

The old Man nodded and trudged back toward town. Narvik, one of Lorrodrig's longtime intimates, called to Denarra from the barge.

"Boat's packed; time to cast off."

The Strangeling picked up the bag with her few clothes and a week's dry rations and headed to the loading plank. But there was a commotion behind her, an angry shout and a flood of curses. She turned to see the Colonel's horse rearing and bucking, and Pontepael running at full speed toward the dock. When he reached her, he swung her into his arms, kissed her hard, and said, "I'll find you again, sweets. I promise, I'll find you!"

And then he was gone, back to the predictable patterns and sluggish currents of life in Jawbone Crossing, a life he hated, but one he accepted in order to give her the life they'd so often dreamed about. She stood on the threshold of a world far bigger and far more frightening than she'd ever imagined, and she lingered on the edge, watching Pontepael's shadow disappear against the town's looming darkness.

She had this one chance, a gift of love to her from him. He'd loved her when she was Ander, and he loved her now. It was a gift she wouldn't waste. She'd embrace this new life and all its possibilities, for both of them.

"Are ye ready, lass?" Narvik shouted.

"I'm ready for anything!" she called back, shouldering her bag as she sprinted up the gangway to the boat.

Louis Esmé Cruz

my mom names us

my mom names us
flowers and children
of gods, queens and
goddesses though my
dad did, actually.

i ran
away from her
long and thick brown legs
kicking through cut grass
one of the few times
she tried
to spank me,
I just kept moving
my butt
away.
finally she broke down
into laughter
then tears

she kept laughing.
always thought she was kind
of weird
superstitious for the daughter of our Father.

criss-cross fingers this way,
one knock that.
no apparent reason.
mom said so.

if you give a child
a name
old and cloudy from before birth
expect a storm
thick, black and heavy
that won't let even you through.

we move
tired.
birthing babies, mixing medicines.
trying to forget—
i'm trying to not forget.

I want her back now
from before
she went mad,
before the violence broke her.

what did her laughter
sound like then,
what sparkle
in her grey-green eyes?

Carrie House

Kid

I saw my brothers at the barber shop
My dad gave my mom my pigtails, with marble-looking hair ties
At the playground I would take and play with the boys' Hot Wheels
Keep them for several days and then give them back
Boys would fight me, I would punch back, and saw them fall
Then saw them go to the principal's office
I gave upper-cuts, jabs, and side punches
A report card had ". . . should play with girls more often . . ."
Another report card had ". . . boys feel intimidated . . ."
I climbed over the school's brick wall and walked half a mile
through sagebrush before the janitor caught me
I climbed up my parents' fence and my brother peeled me off
and drove me to school
A boy had his older brother fight me
He was three grades above me and I made him cry
While out herding sheep I peed like the guys
We chewed Skoal and had spitting contests on corrugated metal roofs
Carved roads and tunnels into the red sandstone for my Matchbox cars
My brothers would tie me up
I would free myself and track them down through arroyos and cliffs
When I found them I threw stones at them or shot stones at them with
    a slingshot
A brother teased me and I shot him in the ass with a BB gun
My mom bought me a toy Colt 44 gun

It seemed like the real deal; the hammer clicked loud, the pin
    pulled out
releasing the bullet casing for me to inspect, for bullets
I would pop the casing back in and spin, sure sounded like the real
    deal
My jacket had inside pockets
I had guns, rocks, knives, firecrackers, and jerky in my pockets
Us guys would hold secret mini-rodeos
We roped, flanked, and bucked sheep, ponies, and horses
My dad let me work with him
Hoist vehicles, weld steel, and move railroad ties
I learned how to drive a stock and water truck
Cracker Jacks and strawberry soda were the best treats after herding

Qwo-Li Driskill

Pedagogy

*We walk
alongside power, or
through it—carrying
our illnesses, fearing all
giving has gone to
grave.*
    —Deborah Miranda

*. . . I am still learning how to
walk in this world
without getting caught.*
                —Chrystos

I roll out of bed too
late to take a shower
throw on whatever is clean
Each muscle bruises under the
burden of movement

As I drive to class in dawn's dark
I worry about the cancer
cells on my little sister's cervix
My oldest sister's gallstones
The hepatitis C in my father's liver
The most recent accidental carbon monoxide
poisoning that put my mother in bed for days

Pain scrapes my shoulder blades and
I am thinking about how the doctor asked
what country I was from
when I opened my mouth
and how to talk to you about Argument

I am worrying about my friend who can't leave
the house because of toxic air
my partner's depression and HIV

If any of the people I love will be shot in the face by police
      shouted down by priests
                    beaten to death on the way home
If we will get away
          this time

(The odds, darlings, are against us)

I am worrying about how to not get caught in
this world we've written
and if we should talk about Invention or
proofreading this morning

And I know there are marks on your bones
you can't or won't speak
scars whose names you resist
long wars fought on and over your bodies

I know that you are more worried about
finding enough pennies to buy
instant noodles for the week
than the Media Analysis due tomorrow

On the way to class
you are thinking about your mother's cough
           multiplication of cells
                    chemical compounds
what to tell your family that you're learning in college
and if tonight you're gonna say
I love you

You will arrive in class this morning
to a conversation about
ethos
      pathos
         logos
Use words like
    power   privilege   oppression   binary

What does this classroom have to do with you anyway?
What does it have to do with any of us?

I am here because I was tired of eating from garbage cans,
playing my flute, always one foot on the wet Seattle street

You are here because Dad said
or to finally get out of that damn town
or to survive a country
whose tongue yearns
for your blood

This class will not save you
This class will not save any of us

I pray you take some words with you
like sharpened spoons
ferry them away up your sleeves
under your tongues

I pray I can teach you
to saw through
the iron bars
of this country

This country
waiting for us
teeth
just sharpened
this morning

Chrystos. "Crazy Grandpa Whispers." *Not Vanishing*. Vancouver: Press Gang, 1988.
    Miranda, Deborah. "Highway 126." *The Zen of La Llorona*. Cambridge, UK: Salt
Publishing, 2005.

Janet McAdams

Plaza Bocanegra

I am sitting in the Plaza. I am thinking of Bocanegra. I am thinking of her, though this is not the Plaza Bocanegra.

No, Anna thinks, this is the Plaza Grande. Bocanegra's is the little plaza, the Plaza Chica. How fitting, she thinks, and looks up from the letter she is writing. Looks up and knows it is a mistake because she catches the eye of the Traveler. His feet shift nervously in the Jesus sandals he has worn every day since she met him. She has not seen sandals like this since she was fifteen, the early seventies, when everyone she knew had those sandals, long drapey clothes, long drapey hair. She had worn the hair but not the sandals. Her sandals were a prim white, so wrong that one day she wore her best friend Natalie Carter's extra pair even though her heels hung off the ends by an inch and a half. Halfway through the school day when the grit digging into her soles became unbearable, she went in and changed. "You changed your shoes!" Missy Ann Tascadero had exclaimed, exchanging glances with the two interchangeable girls who appeared invariably on Missy's right and left sides.

"*¿Estas escribiendo?*" the Traveler asks. "Are you writing?"

She has met two men since she came to these mountains. Franklin, the drunken painter, whose blue eyes were so rheumy with age and bad health she does not know how he manages the precisely astonishing canvases he produces. She thinks he is twins. She does not know how she ever thought she could be friends with a man who still thought he was the twenty-five-year-old beauty in the self-portrait hanging over his sofa. *Paris 1951.*

Franklin worries a great deal about trees. It does not help that Anna is here because a tree crashed on her house, driving her to Mexico while repairs are made. She wasn't home, didn't even know the tree was there when she returned well past midnight and crawled into bed. Only the next morning, standing in the doorway of the kitchen, did she see the long branching limb of it, reaching like a giant hand into the room, blocking the stove, the refrigerator, barring her entrance. She felt despair about her inability to make coffee but did not take the injury to her house personally.

Franklin worries about trees because of his paintings. Some are in museums, a few in private collections, but the majority of them cover the walls of his sister's large house in Alabama.

Surrounding the house are red oaks, trees with fragile roots. He pleads with his sister to cut the trees down, but she refuses to listen. When he drinks, which is about every other month or so, he calls his sister collect, subjecting her to outrageous long distance charges. He tells his sister that she loves her trees more than his paintings, nature more than art, her husband more than him.

Anna is sure he is correct in all of this.

Anna met Franklin when he beckoned her to his table in the breezeway surrounding the plaza. "Looking for a place to sit down?" he said. "I'll buy you a drink." He was drinking then and she was, too.

The second man, the Traveler, clears his throat.

Anna looks up–there is no helping it. The Traveler is a man avoided instantly by nearly everyone, including the locals who don't like Americans, who find them crude, incomprehensible in their willingness to leave their homes and come here just because it is cheaper. But the Traveler they single out for special disdain.

"*¿Estas escribiendo?*" he asks. He speaks very slowly to her as if she were a child, a not terribly bright child, and then translates, speaking just as slowly. He does not know that she speaks Spanish and imagines that bit by bit he is leading her along the path to bilingualism.

She turns back to her notebook, doodling large doughy faces on the white paper, trying to wait him out.

When he leaves, sliding his fat feet into the Jesus sandals and drawing the cord on a ragged string bag, he turns back cheerfully and says, "*Buena suerta,* or should I say, Good luck?"

The chocolate is stone cold, her mouth sour. It is nothing like the Mexican chocolate they serve in the States. Each day, she sits here writing letters, trying to remember, and she orders the chocolate, hoping it will finally turn into the dark, cinnamon-laced cocoa her grandfather used to buy her in the stockyards in Oklahoma City.

The bougainvillea are lush in the courtyard of the small hotel where she is staying. This country is ridiculously beautiful. She can't imagine telling anyone at home about it and them believing her. Her friends do not travel. When she is home, they will have her over for dinner. Moroccan food or Malaysian—whatever this month's fancy is. They will ask earnest questions: What are *the people* like there? How do they *live* in that country?

But she will have nothing to say, only: This is how I lived, what I ate there, what colors the bougainvillea bloomed in, how the light was especially clear in the mornings when I sat in the square.

Franklin comes into the tiny courtyard, squinting and looking around. He carries a large, padded envelope. When he sees Anna, alone at one of the wrought iron tables, he comes over. "The photos," he says, perching on the delicate chair next to her, taking out the snapshots of the paintings he finished over the summer. She is only allowed to look at them with Franklin. He turns them over, one by one, offering explanations, asking her what she thinks, explaining the errors in her responses when she ventures them. His breath is yeasty on her neck. The last painting shows a thick young man with a knapsack. Religious icons are embedded in the landscape he crosses.

The thick young man is the Traveler. "Why?" she asks Franklin.

But Franklin only shrugs. "He's always looking for that Buddhist temple." In the painting, the young man's face is radiant, the source of light untraceable.

But there is no Buddhist temple, Anna thinks, after Franklin has packed his photos and left, talking a little to himself, "Glad you liked the one of Circe." Anna hadn't realized it was Circe.

"I know what you could write a story about," the Traveler coughs gently. "*Yo conozco lo que usted—tu—podría escribir . . .*"—he hesitates— "*escribirlo de un cuento.*"

Anna waits. Across the square she can see the tree where the Spanish shot the young Gertrudis Bocanegra. It was hewn off at the top, barely alive, the black from the iron fence around it protecting the bullet hole laced trunk. "What?" she asks.

She tries to see the radiance in the Traveler's sweat-streaked pale face. "*Un hombre,*" he says, wiping the sweat with the dirty sleeve of his gauze shirt. "Okay," he wipes his nose, his ears, his hairline. "I'm going to tell you in English, okay?"

Anna nods. The mountains ring the town like a halo, their summits white against the nearly turquoise sky. If I were rich I would stay here forever, she thinks. If I could live without love. If.

"This is a true story," he says. Anna closes her eyes and leans back. "Are you listening?" he asks and she nods. As he begins, she sees not the unhappy man, thousands of miles from a home she cannot imagine, but the man from Franklin's painting. As he crosses the canvas landscape, the icons soften, the Catholic Jesus sits up from his cross as if it were a soft bed. His long face grows rounder, the blood on it fading to a becoming flush. The marble Buddha unbends his cramped legs and stands tall as a tree. Saint Lucy replaces her two gray eyes and looks around at the bright world, at Anna and the Traveler in their wicker chairs. The Traveler's face is so full of light it shines through the stammered words of the tale he is spinning. So light it lifts them both, into the clean air, suspending them in a moment that is not this foreign country and not the land they would call home.

Daniel David Moses

The Ends of a Picnic

Oh you're black and lucky, bird, strutting through the grass
out into the sun—and away from an impasse
in conversation, from words gone blue, too sour
in the heat, ever to chew on, let alone eat.

We could be lucky too or bright with a slew of
picnic fixings to squeeze in lieu into our beaks.
How nice to have pre-sliced cheese and cold cuts to share,
I've always said. How nice to break bread. You don't need

knives to—and chance is with us, since we did forget
to bring a blade along into the shade today
where the green of lawns won't be cutting off any
arteries. Wit's evident too in these far too

few sweet grapes included on the menu. Or is
that irony one only I have the taste for?
We're sharing the relative calm of a blanket
spread out in the public sun but the appetites,

yes, the vocabulary, we held in common
are gone or in need of translation. Is that why
you're here, you dark and winged thing, to bring some sense
back into our sentences, our heads? To feed off

all the clever words we said? To take them up through
the haze of poplar fluff and leave the silences
we're waiting in white as the face of the pond is
under a cover of the stuff? No reflections

show up there or here unless the wind or we stir
—and who dares at these temperatures? Only you
and that one young man who also strutted over
the grass, just as cocky as that red and yellow off

your wings. He made the trek all the way uphill out
of the shade and now, bending over the spouting
fountain there, like the sun thirsty on his brown skin
for bright salt, he begins sucking up that jet as

if it really were a spring, really were that sort
of first ever clear flowing, like the one that once
upon a time got the two of us going, yes,
unafraid to go along on this escapade.

PART FOUR

Wild/Flowers

Cheryl Savageau

Where I Want Them

on the lids of my eyes on the nape
of my neck across the top of my
shoulder down the side of my
arm grazing the hair and over the
knuckle of each finger and then
the fingertips one at a time in
the center of my palm on the tender
inside of my forearm in the crease
of my underarm the hollow of my
throat between my breasts circling
each nipple circling my navel following
the line of my backbone to the small
of my back on the mound of each
cheek on the tender underside of my
ass on the backs of my knees on the
inside of my thighs on the lips of the
flower where you will find me
trembling

M. Carmen Lane

Remember

SHE BOUGHT THOSE PANTIES FOR YOU

for J.

If you told your self the truth you would remember it differently. You knew exactly what she wanted when she asked you to take her home. You wanted to see the interior of her longhouse—be less than 20 feet from her bed. You wanted to touch her interior. Muthafucka you froze. You saw the red lace bra and panties removed from that bag and knew she bought them for you. She who embodied all that you had ever wanted in a woman, she who embodied all you had ever wanted in your wife. *If you told your self the truth* you waited and waited hoping your heart would grow big enough and fearless enough to grab her up into your arms. Instead you allowed her to throw her self into you over and again until she knew just what kind of pussy you were. What kind of pussy you are. You talk big game and puff out that butch chest of yours, but she wanted you to be her man. She prayed for you to be the husband she had ached for all her life. You knew you didn't know how to do that after the fiasco with that other femme from San Francisco. Well, she just wasn't that into you anyway. *If you told your self the truth* you would not have told her you were afraid, you would have told her that you didn't know how to be an Indian Man. You would have told her that there was much for you to learn in order to be a good Indian Man to her or you would've just tapped that ass. No, *if you told your self the truth* you would have told her you knew you were brought to her by the Spirits and that you knew you were her husband and felt that knowing deeply in your bones and heart; deep in your own soul down, even deeper still, straight into the Earth, straight up into the Sky. But, while you are no longer christian and those Jesus ethics you've critiqued all those years

194

fluttered around in your lungs and bubbled up in your belly, well, you done punk'd your self out of a wife. Damn, all of that after her father came and taught you everything you ever needed to know to love her right. *sekon Deer/Man, I have not taken you for granted. I watched crappy "Thunderheart" like you asked and figured it all out . . . nya:weh.* This is the difference between being a butch Black lesbian and a Two-Spirit Indian Man. Not *nadleeh* or *winkte* (misogynist academics always focus on the men who are women) but a Man Spirit with big Black Woman titties and a flat Indian ass. Remember now, when she would say "You're a man." *If you told your self the truth* it was not her fear of your female body that caused those words to come from her lips, nor was it homophobia or naiveté. It was a naming of the connection between her femme body and your man heart. She recognized it and you didn't. She acknowledged it and you didn't. She loved it and you did not. Instead your macho ass chose to compete with her husband. It wasn't even him that you had to worry about. You always thought when she called you her other husband that she was putting you in relationship to him. Nope. Funny what you learn when you begin to listen and talk with the Ancestors. Other spirits begin to show up too. They're jealous that you can walk between worlds and they cannot. When you gon' learn not just to listen but to walk this Red Road? Shit, *if you told your self the truth* . . . what kind of man could you become? Didn't she buy those panties for you?

Maurice Kenny

Naughty Probably

I have loved always
                    plums
round and purple
touched lightly by morning dew
cold to the tongue's
                    first lick
I could never wait for
                    jam
for breakfast toast
sweet to lips
            palate
as juice rounds down
                    the mouth

I have loved always
                    plums
significant
to boyhood
as manhood rises to claim
growing hair on the chin
and whiskers tickle

plums don't last long
they hang a day
                    and

then wither over night
until not even a wild stag
will push away the dark
to steal a bite

I have loved always plums

Sarah Tsigeyu Sharp

Rebirth

We etch home into the palms of our hands
lift them toward the moon, that they might be
magnified by her glory
Dangle feet over boulders in the river
Close eyes tight, pretend these are our homelands

Remember past tanglings of spit
and weavings of skin that brought us here,
birthed us, brought honey to our trembling lips,
food and sweetness for the fight ahead.
Today is a good day to cry.

Your eyes like an amber cavern in a thunderstorm
and as bright as the day is long
I shudder under you as your tongue teaches my
body to speak
Taíno, Carib, Guanahatabey, español y poco niño ingles
You are a dialect unto yourself.

I was the farthest East I'd ever been,
more than 2900 miles from home
you, redefining the word with your small hands

I could push sand into your mouth to stifle my terror
lest you speak,

break me into bits and I should   tumble down your
throat,   the end of me
But you   and the Taíno sun are inside me now,
for good

Then, 41000 feet in the sky, heading steadily away
from you
I cherish the flush/of my lust
      You grated me my own heat, bottled tight inside
my frigid, North American heart,
a product of the colonization of my people

We were once as wild as you/
       some of us still are
some of us just need a little help from our liberated kin
       thus, I name you such:
Kin, Sibling in Struggle

I knew the day would come when indigenous lifts
indigenous closer to the sun,
I just never could have guessed it would be like this:
      you, all eyes and hands and tongue
You are acts of gods exiled long ago
      from this, our fertile earth

You and I
a dialogue
of rebirth

Maurice Kenny

Sargent: Drawing of Nicola D'Inverno

Accused of pornography . . .
proving dull minds blind . . .
yet real, sensual, could
add sensitive; a finger
might reach and
touch a slack penis,
Nicola's nipple, his
shadowed lip, leg
bent at the knee.

The use of imagination:
charcoal on cream paper, or blue;
suggestion of warm lines, flesh
caressed by extraordinary art.

(Where does Nicola stare!
into what dream, fantasy,
eye which might return dreamy
glances and ease the labor
of modeling his naked body . . .
though we should say nude
as naked is definitely
pornographic and to be hidden,
draped from innocent eyes

which might find pleasure in
Nicola's particular
handsomeness . . . even the small
moustache and the curls of
his black flowing hair,
the ageless face that will
remain youthfully nineteen
until the last winds blow and sun
refuses to rise and recognize his
penis which folds between his thighs.
Or enjoy Sargent's art.)

Or another watercolor on paper
where groin and loin are denied
to curious eyes by red drapery.
But the beauty . . . can we use such a word
when speaking of a male nude,
the exquisite dedication is not
only male but Biblical which indeed
legalizes the nudity. Caravaggio
would have no problem with this
figure, nor would Bacon shiver.

James Thomas Stevens

St. James Lake

On a footbridge
crossing
      the lake toward
            Horse Guards Road,
I stop to listen
as dim twitterings grow to a deafening roar.

This is how the body is,
suddenly aware of its own dull thud.

Knowing, how our own song
completes the chorus. How each preened park-goer
carries a specific yet woefully similar call,
            Sanctuary.

You, singing beautifully in churches and town squares.
Us, humming in harmony once
beneath arched vaults above the *Isère.*

I can never think far from the heart.

Nearing Birdcage Walk,
I envision the intricate cage of your ribs at night.

Imagine the frightened flocks we carry:

Grey Wagtail
Swan

Shoveler
Pelican
Raven
Golden Eye

Oh plucking Zeus. Oh Ganymede. Oh frightened furies flying
    breakneck
in our chests.

How it all becomes fantastical, here.

All elephants and castles, chalk farms and canaries. All mile ends
and mudchutes. All circus.

Birdkeep of a brain,
there must be someone
watching out
            for the heart.

Between that Charybdian eye and Buckingham,
we near Duck Island, and of a sudden
                            it appears.

The birdkeeper's cottage.
Its thatched roof hanging
                    impossibly heavy.

How idyllic, how monstrous
the responsibility for these many birds.

I could live here, I say.
I could live here too.

I hear, *with*, take flight. Its gently upturned wings lifting from water.

Turning to go to sleep at night, you offer your sore shoulder,
and in the strain of muscle beneath my thumbs, I note its avian blade.

Qwo-Li Driskill

Sonnet for Izzy

You just never know what exactly he'll knit:
A monogram scarf, or tomorrow a sweater,
a hat, shawl, or blanket—if sassy, a fetter
to bind his limp wrists. Or a frock fit to flit
in and show off those legs. In Gainsborough blue
he'll stitch and he'll weave, such a brilliant, coy
cover for hot scenarios planned. Such a naughty boy
with tattooed chest and makeup in genderfuck hues,
he giggles demurely, new clutch in hand. Oh, how cute
he is when he asks for a tussle or a serious spank
from boys who then plot what best ways to flank
his thin waist and ways to impress through vigor and brute.
From connoisseur of bath porn to weaver of fabric:
his warp spun from sin, his weft twisted from maverick.

Maurice Kenny

Visiting San Francisco

Just yesterday, like a dog, I pissed
on the grass in Dolores Park,
reclaimed California for Indians
as it had been stolen from us years
ago. A passing lesbian poet frowned
on my heroism and told me where to go.
I gave her a robin feather, flipped
her off, and drove away to Papalote's
in the Mission for burritos
with my friends while tightly
clutching a $10.00 bag of candy
purchased in Sausalito, most
happy another day was sun
and temporarily without
expected Pacific morning fog.

My little criminal act produced
relief and political contentment.

Chip Livingston

Man Country

north of Little Rock is famous they told me
the sentence sold through that that I'd heard
after the printed muscles switched lengthwise
and the horniest straightened
rocked the webbing St. John netted
the map graphing   *What I mean is I'm*
and facing speculation still in his favor
narrowly betting a closing argument pick-up
cloudless semi-private and clean-shaven
gauge stilled and God marking his territory
ushering conditions   conveniences shuttering
the guaranteed hand   my hand

Daniel David Moses

How to Make a Fish Sweat

Jigging overhead through the haze the metal of
stars, so far away, won't lure more than eyes from bed.

The rest of our bodies, spread out at the bottom
of the night, even up on the seventeenth floor,

dive after the ice in the depths of tall, empty
glasses, searching for an alcohol clear shiver.

We find instead a stir in the heavy water
we're made of, a hot flow of salt rising into

muscles, nostrils, the shining cheeks of our faces.
The current the fan on the sill supplies never

will dry up the one in our skins. Oh our tongues shine
silver with the taste, spooning the submarine night.

Malea Powell

forgiveness on a november sunday

for curry

sleeping   you breathe, the long angles of your thighs taut with
    golden light
one arm across your chest   long fingers resting
i could lift that hand,   invite you upstairs that sun-drenched
    white-sheeted bed
we'd generate a slow-burning sun of our own
would you lick my mouth breasts belly   drink me slow, tongue
    insistent
again and again and again
    sweet forgiveness
i could kneel beside you lower my head   a dream fire to awaken
    you
straddle your thighs   we could soak up the sun in me   rising
    on you
would you swirl me in and around hands heart   paint stars against
    my closed eyes
again and again and again
    sweet forgiveness
instead you wake slowly   catch me watching   writing
read me aloud kiss me white-sun-hot skin going molten   light
strip me bare   a leaf   fluttering in this relentless autumn gold
    spilling
spinning   again
sweet forgiveness

Michael Koby

Calumet Cemetery

And we are alive here
walking round granite teeth
snug in the wet green jaw

The trees, obelisks
point up, up, up
toward the golden crown of morning

And I am trying to be honest;
having watched that movie last night
with you, comfortable on our couch
Chinese lantern burning—

Once I wanted a long box
and after that fancy passed
a rock-n-roll band
a family (so simple)

And this is all
I am cut out to do
keep on trying till 3:12 a.m.
to write it all down

One day I will be able to write a poem that says *I love*

Because I do—
beside this window

our window
overlooking this field of gray stones
—need to say
(hush) I (can't write it)
am glad we found this blue paint
warm, bold color
that says we are here

We English china cups, our little white mouths
(the art of survival!)
still set upon the floor
after all this winter's parties
a considerable gesture
in spite of ourselves.

Deborah Miranda

Clementines

Work the skin off in a ragged spiral,
separate flare from the pale sunrise within.
Gather up the long curl of rind,
turn it tight and snug, coy center peeking out
from swirled petals. Make a Clementine rose,
leave it like a love letter on the table.
Let your thumbs find the top dimple, apply pressure.
Not sudden, not hesitant, but cleanly.
Know the joy of secret compartments.
Raise the Clementine's luminous body
on the tips of your fingers, moist, undressed:
with your strong teeth, neatly pluck the first
sacrificial half-moon from its sisters
with dreamy dedication:
tongue this plump flame till it bursts,
a lush firecracker in the dark.

Source Credits

The editors and the University of Arizona Press are grateful for permission to reprint the following works:

Paula Gunn Allen, "Some Like Indians Endure," from *Life Is a Fatal Disease: Collected Poems 1962–1995* (West End Press, 1997). Copyright © 1997 by Paula Gunn Allen. Reprinted with the permission of West End Press, Albuquerque, New Mexico.

Qwo-Li Driskill, "Chantway for F.C.," from *Walking with Ghosts* (Salt Publishing, 2005). Reprinted by permission of Salt Publishing.

Janice Gould, "Indian Mascot, 1959" and "We Could Not Forget," from *Doubters and Dreamers* (University of Arizona Press, 2011). Reprinted by permission of University of Arizona Press.

Daniel Heath Justice, "Ander's Awakening," from *W'daub Awae/Speaking True: A Kegedonce Press Anthology* (Kegedonce Press, 2010). Reprinted by permission of the author.

Maurice Kenny, "Sargent: Drawing of Nicola D'Inverno," from *Connotations*. Copyright © 2008 by Maurice Kenny. Reprinted with the permission of White Pine Press, www.whitepine.org. "Visiting San Francisco," from *North Country Literary Magazine* (SUNY–Potsdam, 2008). Reprinted by permission of the author.

Michael Koby, "Santa Claus, Indiana" and "The Witch's House," from *F News Magazine* (the School and Museum of the Art Institute of Chicago, 2004). Reprinted by permission of the author.

Chip Livingston, "Ghost Dance," from *Boulder Planet* (n.d.). Reprinted by permission of the author.

Janet McAdams, "Plaza Bocanegra," from *FemSpec* 2.2 (2001). Reprinted by permission of *FemSpec*.

Daniel David Moses, "Ballad of the Raft" (as "Ballad of the Drowned Heart"), from *Prism International* 26.3 (spring 1988). Reprinted by permission of the author.

"Gray's Sea Change," from *Absinthe* 7.2 (winter 1994). Reprinted by permission of the author. "How to Make a Fish Sweat," from *Prairie Fire* 22.3 (autumn 2001). Reprinted by permission of the author. "Lament Under the Moon," from *Returning the Gift: Poetry and Prose from the First North American Native Writers' Festival* (University of Arizona Press, 1994). Reprinted by permission of the author. "The Ends of a Picnic," from *Siolence: Poets on Women, Violence, and Silence* (Quarry Press, 1998). Reprinted by permission of the author.

Malea Powell, "real Indians," from *Native Realities* 3.2 (spring 2003). Reprinted by permission of the author.

Cheryl Savageau, "Deep Winter" and "Where I Want Them," from *Mother/Land* (Salt Publishing, 2006). Reprinted by permission of Salt Publishing.

James Thomas Stevens, "Thames," "St. James Lake," and "Regent's Canal," from *Bulle/Chimere* (First Intensity Press, 2006). Reprinted by permission of First Intensity Press.

Dan Taulapapa McMullin, "A Drag Queen Named Pipi," "Jerry, Sheree, and the Eel," and "The Act of Memory in Laguna California," from *A Drag Queen Named Pipi* (Tinfish Press, 2004). Reprinted by permission of Tinfish Press.

Craig S. Womack, "The King of the Tie-snakes," from *Drowning in Fire* (University of Arizona Press, 2001). Reprinted by permission of the University of Arizona Press.

About the Contributors

Indira Allegra is a writer and interdisciplinary artist, representing poetry and creative writing in video, digital photography, and fiber arts. She is concerned with themes of emotional intimacy, displacement, and states of hyper-awareness. Her experimental video poem, *Blue Covers*, has screened at festivals and events both nationally and internationally. In 2008, she co-facilitated the artistic vision of performance project *Sins Invalid*, a re/view of embodiment for artists exploring intersections of sexuality and disability. Allegra will share artistic directorship for *Artists against Rape* in 2012. Her writing has appeared in *Rivets Literary Magazine, Make/Shift Magazine*, the 2008 *Artists against Rape Chapbook*, and *Wordgathering*, an online journal of disability poetry. She has forthcoming work in *Dear Sister*, an anthology of letters and artworks dedicated to survivors of sexual violence from other survivors and their allies. She is of African, Tsalagi, and Irish descent. More information can be found at indiraallegra.com and bluecovers.wordpress.com.

Paula Gunn Allen was a foremost voice in Native Studies, and was one of the first Native writers to publicly identify herself and her work as queer. Both her father's Lebanese and her mother's Laguna Pueblo–Métis–Scot heritages shaped her critical and creative vision. Her novel *The Woman Who Owned the Shadows* (1983) was the first novel to have a queer indigenous protagonist. *The Sacred Hoop: Recovering the Feminine in American Indian Traditions* (1986), a collection of critical essays, is a cornerstone in the study of American Indian culture and gender. Her 2004 work of scholarship, *Pocahontas: Medicine Woman, Spy, Entrepreneur, Diplomat,* received a Pulitzer Prize nomination. In addition to her work as a scholar and novelist, she was a prolific poet who published six volumes of poetry, including *Life Is a Fatal Disease: Collected Poems 1962–1995* (1997) and *Skins and Bones* (1988). Her last book of poetry, *America the Beautiful,* was published posthumously in 2010. Allen passed away on May 29, 2008, at her home in Ft. Bragg, California, after a long battle with illness.

Louis Esmé Cruz (Mi'kmaq/Acadian and Irish) is an educator, writer, and visual artist living in Mississauga New Credit Territory, whose work appears in *Scars Tell Stories: A Queer and Trans (Dis)Ability Zine* (2007); the Redwire Native Youth Media Project (2008, 2010); *GLQ: A Journal of Lesbian and Gay Studies,* "Sexuality, Nationality, Indigeneity," edited by Daniel Heath Justice, Mark Rifkin, and Bethany Schneider (2010); *Protecting the Circle: Aboriginal Men Ending Violence against Women* (2010); and *Feminism FOR REAL: Deconstructing the Academic Industrial Complex of Feminism* (2011). Cruz also co-curated *Two-Spirit People: A (Re)Weaving* (2004), *Dirty Gender Secrets* (2005), and *That Indian Show* (2006).

Qwo-Li Driskill is a non-citizen Cherokee Asegi/Two-Spirit/Queer activist, writer, and performer, author of *Walking with Ghosts: Poems* (2005), and co-editor (with Chris Finley, Brian Joseph Gilley, and Scott Lauria Morgensen) of *Queer Indigenous Studies: Critical Interventions in Theory, Politics, and Literature* (2011). S/he is currently an assistant professor in the Department of English at Texas A&M University.

Laura M. Furlan is a Native Chicagoan and an adopted mixed-blood, of Chiricahua Apache, Osage, and Cherokee heritage. She is assistant professor of English at the University of Massachusetts Amherst. Her poetry and creative nonfiction have appeared in *Yellow Medicine Review* and *Sentence.* Furlan lives with her wife and two dogs in Sunderland, Massachusetts.

Janice Gould (Concow) is an assistant professor in Women's and Ethnic Studies at the University of Colorado in Colorado Springs, where she is developing a concentration in Native American Studies for her program. Gould's academic honors include fellowships from the Ford Foundation and the Roothbert Foundation, as well as scholarships from the Association of Research Libraries and the University of Arizona's Knowledge River Program. Her poems and essays have been published in several journals and anthologies. She is the author of three books of poetry, *Beneath My Heart* (1990), *Earthquake Weather* (1996), and *Doubters and Dreamers* (2011), and of an artbook/chapbook, *Alphabet* (1996). With Dean Rader she co-edited *Speak to Me Words: Essays on Contemporary American Indian Poetry* (2003), the first full-length study to document the contributions of Native American poets to the American canon of literature.

Carrie House works in Geographic Information Systems for the Navajo Nation. Her Diné clans are Kinyaa'aanii–Towering Rock House people born for Ch'eehdighahii–Turtle (Oneida Iroquois); maternal grandfather Tsenjikini—Honey-combed Rock people; paternal grandfather Tlizílani—Many Goats people. House wrote, directed, and produced an animation, *Two Embrace* (2009), a voyage into the history of the colonization of the Americas, viewable on NativeOut.org. His poems were part of the Traveling Poetry Gallery, SunTran bus, Albuquerque, and Magnificio, Albuquerque Festival of the Arts, April 1999. House is a contributor to the volume *Two-Spirit People: Native American Gender Identity, Sexuality, and Spirituality* (1997), edited by Sue-Ellen Jacobs, Wesley Thomas, and Sabine Lang. He lives on his ancestral homeland, working toward an organic farm and ranch. He guest lectured for the late Joseph Epes Brown, Religious Studies professor at the University of Montana. She and her late brother, Conrad House, originated the term "balancing factors" to describe indigenous gay people for her media projects. House states, "We are significant balancing factors in the cosmos and world we live in."

Daniel Heath Justice is a Colorado-born Canadian citizen of the Cherokee Nation. Raised in the Rocky Mountain mining town of Victor, Colorado, he now lives with his husband, mother-in-law, and two dogs near the shores of Georgian Bay in Ontario. Justice teaches Aboriginal Literatures and Aboriginal Studies at the University of Toronto. In addition to numerous publications of Native literary criticism, he is the author of *Our Fire Survives the Storm: A Cherokee Literary History* (2006) and an indigenous epic fantasy novel, *The Way of Thorn and Thunder: The Kynship Chronicles* (2011), which features as a major character the protagonist of his story for this collection. His current work includes a cultural history of badgers and a collection of essays tentatively titled "In Search of the Last Cherokee Princess: Literature, Belonging, Desire."

Maurice Kenny has been co-editor of the literary review magazine *Contact/II* and the editor/publisher of Strawberry Press. He has also been poetry editor of *Adironac Magazine,* poet-in-residence at North Country Community College, and visiting professor at the University of Oklahoma–Norman, the En'owkin Center at the University of Victoria, and Paul Smith's College. He is currently on the faculty, as writer-in-residence, of SUNY–Potsdam. Kenny's work has been published in numerous journals, including *Trends, Callaloo, World Literature Today, American Indian Quarterly,* and *Blue Cloud Quarterly,* as well as *Saturday Review* and the *New York Times. The Mama Poems* (1984) received the American Book Award in 1984. The *Bloomsbury Review* cited *Wounds Beneath the Flesh,* edited by Kenny, as best anthology of 1983. *Blackrobe: Issac Jogues* (1982) was nominated for the 1982 Pulitzer Prize in Poetry; *Between Two Rivers* (1987) was nominated for the 1987 Pulitzer Prize in Poetry. In 1996, *On Second Thought* (1995) was a finalist for the Oklahoma Book Award in fiction and the National Book Award. Kenny also published two important collections of poetry, *Tekonwatonti: Molly Brant* (1992) and *Carving Hawk* (2008). In 2000, he received the Elder Recognition Award from the Wordcraft Circle of Native Writers and Storytellers. He is the recipient of a National Public Radio Award for Broadcasting. Kenny presently lives in Potsdam, New York.

Michael Koby is a two-spirit artist and writer of French–Irish–Eastern Cherokee descent. He was born and raised in the middle of nowhere, the small towns and swamps between Indiana's steel mills and farms. His work deals with the insecurities, quirkiness, and invisibility of the townspeople and his own adolescence. He is still the same fourteen-year-old girl trying hard to be cool, but always failing. He currently lives in Santa Fe with his partner, the writer Gregory Brown.

M. Carmen Lane is Haudenosaunee, a two-spirit black lesbian of Mohawk/Tuscarora descent who recently tracked her African indigeneity to the shores of Angola, Guinea-Bissau, Senegal, and Sierra Leone. Lane is an artist, anti-oppression educator, social change consultant, and writer living (for the first time) in Three Fires Territory.

Jaynie Lara (Weye Hlapsi) is a two-spirit woman of the Yaqui nation and Mexican American. She has performed and read her poetry at numerous two-spirit and LGBTQ events in the San Francisco Bay area for a number of years. Lara has been writing poetry since the age of twelve, and each year, she says, her writings grow deeper with the wisdom of life. She has been a community activist for more than twenty-five years, is a board member for the Intertribal Friendship House and Native American AIDS Project, and is a former board member and current member of BAAITS (Bay Area American Indian Two Spirits). She drums and sings with Sweet Medicine Drum, an all–Native American drum circle, which recently played for the Council of 13 Indigenous Grandmothers at the Grace Cathedral in San Francisco and Sedona, Arizona. She currently is teaching traditional Native songs to the two-spirit community.

Chip Livingston is two-spirit, Muscogee Creek, and the author of the chapbook *ALARUM* (2007) and the poetry collection *Museum of False Starts* (2010). Individual poems and stories have appeared in *Barrow Street*, *McSweeney's*, *New American Writing*, *Yellow Medicine Review*, *Red Ink*, and *Ploughshares*. Livingston was born on the Florida/Alabama border but now lives in New York City and Montevideo, Uruguay.

Luna Maia is a San Francisco–based Yaqui mestiza queer poet who writes about issues of mixed heritage, feminism, and gender identity. He has been featured at cafés, libraries, bookstores, and universities throughout the San Francisco Bay area as well as in Tucson and Los Angeles. She performed for four consecutive years in Queer Cultural Center's National Queer Arts Festival and received an honorable mention for the Xochiquetzali Poetry Award in 2008 as well as a 2008 Individual Artist Native American Cultural Equity Grant from the San Francisco Arts Commission.

Janet McAdams is a mixed-blood writer of Creek, Irish, and Scottish ancestry. She is the author of two collections of poetry, *The Island of Lost Luggage* (2000), which won the 1999 Diane Decorah First Book Award from the Native Writers' Circle of America and the 2001 American Book Award, and *Feral* (2007). She is co-editor, with Geary Hobson and Kathryn Walkiewicz, of the anthology *The People Who Stayed: Southeastern Indian Writing after Removal* (2010). Her novel, *Red Weather*, is forthcoming. In 2005, she founded the Earthworks Book Series of Indigenous Writing, which she edits for Salt Publishing. She teaches indigenous literature, environmental literature, and creative writing at Kenyon College.

Deborah Miranda is a two-spirit Ohlone-Costanoan Esselen Nation/Chumash poet and scholar, currently an associate professor of English at Washington and Lee University in Lexington, Virginia, where she teaches creative writing, Native Literatures, American Ethnic Literatures, Women's Literatures, and "The Bad Girl's Guide to the Open Road: American

Women's Travel Literature," a composition course for first-year students. She has published two poetry collections, *Indian Cartography* (1999) and *The Zen of La Llorona* (2005); forthcoming books are *Bad Indians: A Tribal Memoir* and *Raised by Humans: Poems*.

Daniel David Moses is a Delaware from the Six Nations lands in southern Ontario, Canada. Playwright, poet, essayist, and teacher, he holds an honors BA from York University and an MFA from the University of British Columbia. His works for the theater include his first, *Coyote City* (1990), a nominee for the 1991 Governor General's Literary Award for Drama; his best-known play, *Almighty Voice and His Wife* (1992); and *The Indian Medicine Shows* (1995), a winner of the James Buller Memorial Award for Excellence in Aboriginal Theatre. He is also the author of *Delicate Bodies* (1980) and *"Sixteen Jesuses": Poems* (2000) and co-editor of three editions of Oxford University Press's *An Anthology of Canadian Native Literature in English* (1992, 1998, 2005). His most recent publications are *Pursued by a Bear: Talks, Monologues and Tales* (2005); *Kyotopolis* (2008); and *River Range: Poems* (2009), a CD with original music by David Deleary. His honors include the Harbourfront Festival Prize, a Harold Award, a Chalmers Fellowship, and being short-listed for the 2005 Siminovitch Award. He teaches as an associate professor in the Department of Drama at Queen's University, Kingston, Ontario.

D. M. O'Brien, aka Doe, grew up in Moosonee, Ontario. She is of mixed blood—her mother is Omushkego Cree and her father was second-generation Irish Canadian. She is currently busy in the Greater Toronto area as a regional outreach worker, writing more short stories, and raising her two children, with her wife, Nancy. In 2008, she wrote the second edition of the "Two Spirit Women" booklet, which shares the experiences of two-spirit women from the past to the present.

Malea Powell is a mixed-blood of Indiana Miami, Eastern Shawnee, and Euro-American ancestry. She is an associate professor of Writing, Rhetoric, and American Culture at Michigan State University, former director of the Rhetoric and Writing Graduate Program, and a faculty member in American Indian Studies. Powell is the associate chair of the Conference on College Composition and Communication, former editor of *SAIL: Studies in American Indian Literatures*, and former associate national director of the Wordcraft Circle of Native Writers and Storytellers. Her current scholarly work focuses on American Indian material rhetorics and the degree to which these "everyday" arts are critical to understanding our written rhetorical traditions. She is at work on a book manuscript, "Rhetorical Powwows," which examines the continuum of indigenous rhetorical production, and on a critical memoir, "The X-Blood Files." In her spare time, she serves on the advisory board of the National Center for Great Lakes Native American Cultures in Portland, Indiana; hangs out with crazy Native women artists and poets; does beadwork; and writes romance novels.

Cheryl Savageau is an Abenaki poet. She has been awarded fellowships in poetry from the National Endowment for the Arts and the Massachusetts Artists Foundation, and her book of poems *Dirt Road Home* (1995) was a finalist for the Paterson Poetry Prize. Her most recent book is *Mother/ Land* (2006). Savageau also works with textiles, paint, and assemblages and has work in the permanent collection of the Abbe Museum in Bar Harbor, Maine.

Sarah Tsigeyu Sharp is a two-spirit, undocumented Cherokee/Lakota mother of three who strives daily to regift her traditions to her children. She works to preserve endangered Native food and medicine plants for the tribes of her region and teaches folks how to do the same for their own communities. She is a shell-shaker involved in keeping the Sacred Fire of Stomp Dance burning in Tushka Homma, Oklahoma. She is grateful to all those who came before her.

Kim Shuck is a poet, weaver, educator, doer of piles of laundry, planter of seeds, traveler, and child wrangler. She was born in her mother's hometown of San Francisco, one hill away from where she now lives. Her ancestors are Tsalagi, Sauk and Fox, and Polish, for the most part. She earned an MFA degree in weaving in 1998 from San Francisco State University. As a poet, Shuck has read her work around the United States and elsewhere. In 2005, she toured Jordan with an international group of poets in the interest of peace and communication. Shuck reads on local radio frequently. Her visual art has been exhibited both locally and abroad, including a textile show at the National Taiwan Museum in Taipei and the San Jose Art Museum. She consults with museums and galleries on the subjects of Native artwork and community inclusion. She has taught at all levels, and her work with the Exploratorium, a hands-on museum in San Francisco, is included in that museum's "Across Cultures" series. She's been teaching since third grade when she organized and taught a class on crochet. Her work touches on poetry, art, math, storytelling, humor, and whatever else seems useful at the time.

James Thomas Stevens attended the Institute of American Indian Arts and the Jack Kerouac School of Disembodied Poetics at Naropa University and received his MFA from Brown University. Stevens is the author of *Combing the Snakes from His Hair* (2002); *Bulle/Chimère* (2006); *Of Kingdoms and Kangaroo* (2006), with Nicolas A. Destino; *Mohawk/Samoa: Transmigrations* (2006), with Caroline Sinavaiana; *A Bridge Dead in the Water* (2007); and *(dis)Orient* (2008). He is a member of the Akwesasne Mohawk Nation and teaches creative writing at the Institute of American Indian Arts. Stevens lives in Lamy, New Mexico.

Lisa Tatonetti is an associate professor of English and American Ethnic Studies at Kansas State University where she studies, teaches, and publishes on two-spirit literatures. She has essays in *Sherman Alexie: A Collection of Critical Essays* (2010), edited by Jeff Berglund and Jan Roush; *Queer Indigenous Studies: Critical Interventions in Theory, Politics, and Literature* (2011), edited by Qwo-Li Driskill, Chris Finley, Brian Joseph Gilley, and Scott Lauria Morgensen; and the forthcoming *Maurice Kenny: Celebrations of a Mohawk Author*, edited by Penelope Kelsey. She has published in the 2010 special issue of *GLQ: A Journal of Lesbian and Gay Studies*, "Sexuality, Nationality, Indigeneity," edited by Daniel Heath Justice, Mark Rifkin, and Bethany Schneider, as well as in *SAIL: Studies in American Indian Literatures*, *Studies in American Fiction*, *Western Literature*, and *MELUS*. She is currently working on a book project that maps the rise and importance of contemporary two-spirit literature.

Dan Taulapapa McMullin is from the United States Territory of American Samoa (Eastern Samoa) and is a painter, sculptor, multimedia artist, and writer (taulapapa.com). He received a Poets & Writers Award in 1997 from the Writer's Loft, and his short film *Sinalela* won Best Short Film at the Honolulu Rainbow Film Festival in 2002. His work was in solo exhibitions at the De Young Museum, the Gorman Museum, and Fresh Gallery Otara and in group exhibitions at the Bishop Museum, City Gallery of Wellington, Cambridge University, University of the South Pacific, and the United Nations. He is represented in Auckland, Aotearoa–New Zealand, by Okaioceanikarts Gallery. He lives in Laguna, California.

William Raymond Taylor is a descendant of the Osage Nation through his father. A San Francisco–trained social activist, Taylor understands that the personal is political, recognizing the link between the arts and social change. Consequently, he has written and published on Native identity and politics, queer and gender identity, prostitution, fringe and drug culture, HIV/AIDS, mental illness, art history, philosophy, and metaphysics. Taylor's work has been featured in the *James White Review, Suspect Thoughts, Velvet Mafia, Other Magazine, Prosodia, Croatan Express,* and *International Journal of Erotica.* His collected works, *Notes from the Periphery: 1991–2009,* was published in 2010.

Joel Waters is an Oglala Lakota (Sioux) poet. His works have appeared in *Red Ink* magazine; *Genocide of the Mind: New Native American Writing* (2003), edited by MariJo Moore and Vine Deloria Jr.; and *Shedding Skins: Four Sioux Poets* (2008), edited by Adrian C. Louis. Waters currently lives and works in Sioux Falls, South Dakota.

Craig Womack (Muscogee Creek) teaches in the English Department at Emory University and is the author of the novel *Drowning in Fire* (2001); author of the critical texts *Red on Red: Native American Literary Separatism* (1999) and *Art as Performance, Story as Criticism: Reflections on Native Literary Aesthetics* (2009); co-author, with Jace Weaver, Robert Warrior, and Lisa Brooks, of *American Indian Literary Nationalism* (2006); and one of twelve co-authors of the critical collection *Reasoning Together: The Native Critics Collective* (2008).